THE CHURCH YEAR

THE CHURCH YEAR

The Celebration of Faith

Sermons, Volume 2

by

ALEXANDER SCHMEMANN

translated from the Russian
by
JOHN A. JILLIONS

TRADITION
BOOKS

ST VLADIMIR'S SEMINARY PRESS
Crestwood, NY 10707–1699
1994

> *The publication of this book has been underwritten through the generosity of Mr. and Mrs. Alexander Hixon.*

Library of Congress Cataloging-in-Publication Data

(Revised for v. 2)
Schmemann, Alexander, 1921-1983
    Translation of: Voskresnye besedy.
    1. Mary, Blessed Virgin, Saint—Sermons. 2. Orthodox Eastern Church—Sermons. 3. Nicene Creed—Sermons. 4. Sermons, Russian—Translations into English. 5. Faith—Sermons. 6. Revelation—Sermons. 7. Church year sermons. I. Title.
BX126.6.S3413 1991   252'.019   91-639
ISBN 0-88141-111-6 (v. 1)
ISBN 0-88141-138-8 (v. 2)

                                                                    CIP

THE CHURCH YEAR
Celebration Of Faith

English language translation
Copyright © 1994

by

ST VLADIMIR'S SEMINARY PRESS

ISBN 0–88141–138–8

PRINTED IN THE UNITED STATES OF AMERICA

Table of Contents

Foreword

Fr. Alexander Schmemann was one of the leading think-
ers and spokesmen of Orthodox Christianity in the
20th century. At the time of his death in 1983, he was
Dean of St Vladimir's Orthodox Theological Seminary, in
Crestwood, New York, where he had been teaching since
coming to the United States from France in 1951. During
those years he spoke widely and published many articles
and books, but perhaps his largest audience and greatest
influence was in the former Soviet Union. Every week, for
almost thirty years, he delivered a series of broadcasts
over Radio Liberty to reflect upon and explain the meaning of Christianity to an audience deprived by a militantly
atheist regime of their freedom to pursue the spiritual
search. This was the Soviet Union that Fr. Schmemann
knew, where all forms of religious discussion and education were outlawed; where "scientific atheism" and anti-
religious propaganda were part of the school curriculum
from kindergarten through college; where all religious
institutions were harassed and humiliated and threatened
into various degrees of cooperation with the state; where
churches, seminaries and monasteries by the thousands
had been desecrated and destroyed; where religion was
strictly monitored by government bureaucrats, confined to

church buildings, and denied any role or presence in
hospitals, prisons, or among the poor; where dissident
priests, believers and human rights advocates were sum-
marily exiled, imprisoned or hospitalized in psychiatric
institutions; where attendance at church services by
young people was viewed as a crime against the state,
and where major church celebrations were regularly
disrupted by gangs of Communist Youth. This was the
Soviet Union which shaped Fr. Schmemann's talks and
to which they were addressed. He never lived to see the
the collapse of Communism, the opening of the
GULAG, free expression of conscience and religion,
and all the other remarkable changes that have taken
place in Russia since 1988. But since then, the full
extent of previous repression has become even more
solidly documented as government files become avail-
able for the first time.

Given the changes that have taken place in the USSR
and throughout the former Communist world since Fr.
Schmemann first delivered his broadcasts, how can these
talks be of more than passing historical interest? How is
the reader of today to understand references to "anti-religious propaganda" and other features of an atheist state
no longer in existence, especially when he or she lives in
a society where religion and spirituality not only are not
repressed, but seem to be thriving, judging simply by the
numbers of churches, temples, mosques, "Higher Power"
self-help groups, New Age groups, and the explosion of
books on do-it-yourself spirituality? The talks are best
appreciated by those who, like Fr. Schmemann, view the
secularism of modern western culture, including religious culture, as a battle for their souls, a battle no less

intense than that of militant atheism. He defined secularism elsewhere not as the negation of God, but the negation of worship. "A modern secularist," in Fr. Schmemann's words, "quite often accepts the idea of God. What, however, he emphatically negates is precisely the sacramentality of man and world." In other words, secularism denies "that the world is an 'epiphany' of God, a means of his revelation, presence and power."[1] Secularism is a world view and consequently a way of life in which the basic aspects of human existence—such as family, education, science, profession, art, etc.—not only are not rooted in or related to religious faith, but in which the very necessity or possibility of such a connection is denied...

> The characteristic feature of the American culture and "way of life" is that it simultaneously accepts religion as something essential to man and denies it as an integrated world view shaping the totality of human existence...[2]

In these talks Fr. Schmemann was combatting the anti-spiritual forces of atheist propaganda. The talks lose none of their force when put in the context of another front of the same war, the front of modern secularism. The first English volume of these talks, *Celebration of Faith: I Believe*, covers faith, revelation and the basic beliefs of Christianity as summarized in the Nicene Creed. The present volume addresses the church year, and the third will be devoted to the place of Mary, the Mother of God, in Christian life and worship.

John A. Jillions

[1] *For the Life of the World*, St Vladimirs's Seminary Press, 1973, pp. 118-134.

[2] "Problems of Orthodoxy in America: III, The Spiritual Problem," *St Vladimir's Seminary Quarterly*, 9:4, 1965.

Part I

Celebration

1

Why Celebrate?

The church year, with its cycle of feasts, begins in September, as it has since ancient times. Almost no one knows or commemorates this, but as autumn begins it is fitting that we reflect on the meaning of church celebrations and what the very words "church year" imply about the Christian understanding of time.

Anti-religious propaganda has expended a lot of effort combating holy days and religious feasts, debunking and denouncing them as fairy tales, lies, primitive myths utterly devoid of meaning in the modern world. Yet, in quantity alone, the pamphlets and brochures of this anti-feast warfare testify eloquently that feasts remain very much alive and how difficult it has proven to uproot and eradicate them from human life. For example, in spite of all the abuse heaped on Christianity, the Gospel and the account of Christ's birth, in spite of efforts to turn the Christmas tree into a "New Year's tree"—in spite of all of this, when the tree is lit on those dark December nights and the star placed on top, it still commemorates the star which shone long ago over a cave in Bethlehem. All of this has been usurped—the star, the tree, the glowing candles reflected so joyfully in children's eyes—but no one has succeeded in turning them into convincing symbols of dialectical materialism and atheism. That is why the enemies of Christianity must resort to cruder measures, as they do on Easter night, mobilizing hordes of Communist Youth. On that one-of-a-kind spring night when Christians celebrate "the feast of feasts" and "the holy day of holy days," the Komsomol disrupts and intimidates worshippers by shouting and swearing to drown out words of incomparable beauty: "Now all is filled with light, heaven and earth and the lower regions. Let the whole world, visible and invisible, celebrate the rising of Christ, in whom we are established..." The Komsomol shouts and mocks, but Easter's light retains its radiance and remains the same source of joy it was a thousand years ago. Opponents of religious celebration have devoted much attention to writing banal pamphlets in an effort to convince us that lies of the most obvious, most transparent sort were somehow capable of controlling people for centuries.

Why not instead reflect more deeply, and ask why it was that for centuries and for literally millions of people, it was the church year which sanctified them and gave meaning to their lives? Why not try to understand the wonderfully organic fabric of feasts, which weave for each season its own unique color, its own unique depth? The light of Christmas, the bright sadness of Lent which imperceptibly is transformed into the joy of Easter, the summer and sun-filled feasts of Ascension and Pentecost, August's profound pre-autumn celebration of Transfiguration and Dormition: are these all fiction? Delusion? Myth? Let's for a moment concede that they are. But if so, why not at least make an attempt to understand what kind of deep approach to life undergirds these "myths"?

For one fact is absolutely clear: the human being cannot live without holidays and feasts, without celebrations. Sociology, and not religious sociology by the way, long ago proved scientifically and objectively that feasts belong to the very deepest, most primitive layer of human life and culture. No society, no civilization has ever existed without feasts. Even anti-religious, militantly atheist society has its feasts and spawns its own cycle of celebrations: the Day of Work, the Day of Women, and so forth—one holiday after another. Even the festal rituals remain: processions, parades, flowers, singing, music, recreation, relaxation, parties and banquets. Therefore, I repeat: don't discredit and debunk feasts as products of religious fabrication and delusion. Instead, consider the phenomenon itself, the very fact of feasts and celebrations in human life. And then reflect on their meaning for human beings. We celebrate all kinds of events, but no matter what it is that gives rise to a particular celebration, what remains constant is the need for celebration. Where does this come from? And what does it say about human nature? These are the questions which must concern us. As I said earlier, we know of no human society, even the most primitive, without feasts and celebrations.

What do we know about these early feasts? Two fundamental observations. First, and most obviously, the feast is part of man's inescapable rhythm of work and rest. In order to live, a person must work. But he cannot work without rest. In every place and culture this gives rise to the rhythm of work and rest. But in addition, rest—the opportunity of not working—is always experienced as a joy. This is the first and most obvious source of celebration. But in the development of feast as feast, there is another more important root: man's need for meaning. Through the feast man gives meaning to work itself, and therefore, to all life. And it is precisely here, in man's absolutely irreppressible need not just for rest, but for joy, for meaning, that we find the true source of celebration and its tenacity in human society. Animals, as well as human beings, live according to the rhythm of work and rest; they too have a physiological need to rest, but it remains for them something strictly physiological, untransformed into the joy of festal celebration.

According to its own logic, based as it is on a materialistic worldview, anti-religious propaganda is correct and consistent when it denounces religious feasts, but incorrect and inconsistent when it replaces them with civic feasts. To be entirely logical and consistent from a materialistic point of view, there can be no feasts whatsoever, only the animal and physiological rhythm of work and rest. Rest is merely the recharging of the organism for new work. And so each day requires so many hours of sleep, each week requires one "day off," each year requires so many weeks of vacation. But the motive for all this is strictly utilitarian: to keep up the organism's strength, its "capacity for productivity."

Primitive man, however, did not merely rest. He celebrated. Exertion and work did not merely alternate with sleep and rest, but "blossomed" into the joyous opportunity of seeing the fruit of one's labor, of giving meaning to that labor, of rejoicing in it. In celebration and feast, labor ceased being a grim treadmill, a fight for survival, an endless chain of days and nights. Instead, labor was given meaning, its results could be contemplated, it became inspired and human. In spite of socialist hymns in praise of Labor, people know that labor inevitably means work, exertion and fatigue. But human beings can accept all this, and indeed transform it, when their work is crowned not simply with material success, but when it becomes a vehicle for freedom, joy and fulness of life. And this is exactly the meaning of the feast at its deepest and most primitive level: man liberating himself from a life chained solely to necessity and unbreakable law. This is why man does not simply rest, he celebrates. This is why feasts and celebrations become the repository and expression of his understanding of life's goals and meanings. And this is why, finally, it is through celebrations, or rather through man in celebration, through *festal man*, that one best appreciates the meaning of various faiths and worldviews. Put another way, "Tell me what you celebrate, and I will tell you who you are..."

2

The Roots of Christian
Celebration: Passover

What does the Christian celebrate? For if it is true that a person expresses himself best and most purely when he is celebrating and joyful; if it is true that religion is first and foremost about joy in God and is therefore about celebration, then Christianity also is best understood through its joy and feasts rather than through abstract dogmatic and theological formulas. Since its earliest days, Christianity, and the Orthodox Church in particular, expressed and embodied its faith, its understanding of the world and its approach to life, through a network of feasts embracing the entire year. Without exaggeration, we can say that the believer lives from feast to feast, and that for him these feasts beautify all time through the comings and goings of each season of the year—fall, winter, spring, summer.

It is not unusual to hear about the negative side of religious feasts: the claim that they go hand in hand with drunkenness, laziness, and so forth. But in evaluating the essence of any occurrence, what must first be examined are not the abuses, but its primary meaning and significance. With religious feasts, this means that it is necessary to speak first from the point of view of how they were designed and intended to be celebrated. Only then, and in defense of this positive meaning, can abuses and short-comings—which are always possible—be addressed.

There is no better introduction to Christian celebration than Easter—or "Pascha"—the feast which the Orthodox Church has always called "the feast of feasts," the source of unique joy for all believers, a joy which can be compared to nothing else. Christians received this feast from ancient Judaism, where as "Passover" [in Greek, *Pascha*] it was the most important religious event of the year. The distinctly Christian meaning of this celebration is best uncovered by tracing its connection—both positive and negative—to its Jewish precursor. From the gospels we know that Christ's passion, the week of his crucifixion and death, coincided with the Jewish Passover. In the gospels' perspective, this coincidence was not accidental. What is the significance of these two events' coming together? What were the Jews celebrating and why did the apostle Paul later call Christ "our Passover," saying, "For Christ, our Passover lamb has been sacrificed" (1 Cor 5:7)? In answering these questions we gradually enter an entire worldview. It may appear archaic to contemporary man with his technology and utilitarian, banal approaches to life; but in reality this worldview corresponds to something eternal, indestructible, and of the greatest importance and depth in the human soul. With this in mind, it is essential to understand just how the layers of meaning in the celebration of Passover gradually developed.

The first stage is rooted in the early nomadic life of the Jews, when they were not farmers, but herders of cattle, sheep and goats. Passover first makes its appearance as a spring celebration of new life, new livestock. This is the origin of the ancient rite of giving thanks by offering a young ram in sacrifice. Here too is the origin of the first ritual of the Jewish Passover, sacrificing the Passover lamb.

The second stage in the development of this feast came with the settlement of Canaan and the beginning of agriculture. Passover then takes on new meaning as the feast of nature's spring renewal, the cosmic triumph of life. But so far, this still concerns only nature and human life as it exists in and through the natural world.

Later, a third layer of meaning is added to Passover, the historical dimension. For man lives not only in natural time but in historical time, within a process that interprets past, present and future and fills with meaning not only the lives of individuals, but humanity as a whole. Several centuries before Christ, Passover becomes the annual commemoration of the Exodus from Egypt, liberation from slavery, the forty-years of wandering in the wilderness, and finally, the entrance into the Promised Land.

But these historical events, through the preaching and teaching of the prophets, gradually grew beyond their original and limited meaning, they broadened to unfold a universal vision. Passover became a celebration of joy in human history, its progression from slavery to freedom, from sadness to joy, from bitter hunger in the desert to the blossoming fruit of the Promised Land. All these different strands are gradually united into one celebration of Passover: nature, history, and finally hope in the coming of God's Kingdom, the Kingdom of peace and love, freedom and happiness. Passover becomes a symbol of human life itself, directed toward a good and joyful conclusion. The triumph of spring foreshadows the final triumph of the cosmos; the commemoration of a past liberation grows into anticipation of a final and complete liberation; and together they reveal to man the ultimate meaning of what exists.

Passover was all of this at the time of Christ, if only as a concept, as an idea. And therefore it is clear why Passover becomes the center of the gospel story, and why everything in which we believe, when we say that we believe in Christ, is so connected to the days of Passover, and finds its key in Passover. Christ proclaimed the Kingdom of God, that very Kingdom which was first announced, first revealed, and continues to be revealed to man by the beauty of creation and nature. Within Spring there lies the symbol and promise of a final and ultimate beauty. Christ proclaimed that Kingdom which man in history has dreamed of and strived toward. And finally, He proclaimed that Kingdom which overcomes all fear and horror of death, dissolution and decay. Christ taught that in him, in his life and especially in his sacrificial death, Passover is completed and fulfilled. It is the Passover or passage for which the whole world has thirsted, the passage from slavery, time, and death to freedom, life, and love. This is precisely the reason Christ is called "our Pascha," why his death on the Jewish Passover brought that feast to completion and filled it with its final and universal meaning, and why his resurrection became the center of Christianity's faith and joy.

3

The First Day of the New Creation

According to the gospels, Christ's resurrection occurred on the first day of the week. In New Testament times, the last and crowning day of the week was Saturday, the seventh day. This was both the day of rest and the day of solemn and joyful praise to God, who is revealed in his Creation. According to the first chapter of Genesis, God completed his creation of the world in six days, and on the seventh day He "rested from all his work" (Gen 2:3). It is important to remember that numbers throughout the ancient world were endowed with deep symbolic and religious significance. Thus the number seven, and therefore the seventh day, came to mean wholeness, completeness, and perfection. The number seven became a symbol of this world and this cosmos which God created, completed and called "very good" (Gen 1:31). The time of this world was also symbolized by seven, in a complete week of seven days.

The numerology of the ancient world seems childish and naive when considered from the pedestrian and joyless perspective of the modern world. The intent here, however, is not to gather converts for numerology, but to foster appreciation for the worldview that stands behind such an approach. The week continues to be seven days, and even the most rational attempts to reform this have for some reason never succeeded. But the significance of "seven," rooted as it is in an "archaic" understanding of time, escapes us, because in our rationalistic pride we refuse to admit the full seriousness and depth of the ancient worldview. In its simplest form, this worldview leads to two fundamental conclusions about man's perception of time. First, man experiences time as cyclical: day follows night, spring follows winter, in an eternal rotation, an eternal cycle of beginning and ending enclosed within time. Through its very cyclic nature, time is an image of completion and of the world as complete and fully connected from beginning to end. Time is thus an image of the world's completeness and wholeness. Life is enclosed within time and fully expresses itself within time: spring, summer, autumn, winter; morning, afternoon, evening, night—all of these are stages of life itself, and each stage is necessary for life to be complete and fulfilled. This is the positive or, in religious terms, cosmic meaning of time, which ancient societies symbolized by the number seven.

However, there is also a negative side to the human experience of time. Time is the most obvious image of slavery and mortality: human beings as well as everything else in the world are enslaved to time and death. There is no escape from time. Deliberately and exactly, time parcels out its allotments to each and leads all that exists towards inescapable death. The writer and philosopher Vladimir Solov'ev expressed this very well in a famous line: "Death and time rule the earth." Wherever time exists, death is always present. Yet time is everywhere, and so death is woven throughout the entire fabric of time.

All of this, the negative and positive aspects of time, are contained within the number seven as understood by the ancient world: the world in its completeness, the world also in its limitation and mortality; life's joy pregnant with the sadness of death. While tearing down these old beliefs and viewing them with contempt from the heights of pseudo-scientific authority, today's ideologues claim to answer humanity's deepest questions. But what is the meaning of life's fluctuations and reversals? Why is joy granted if it is inevitably followed by separation, decay, disappearance and death? The ideologues have no answer, of course, and the happiness they promise will still end in death.

Two thousand years ago, Christianity conquered the world with the joy of Easter, the resurrection. This joy was above all an answer to humanity's perpetual question and grief about life's duality, joy and mortality. It is only if we understand this that we can then appreciate the great importance the first Christians attached to what might otherwise appear to be an inconsequential detail in the gospel account of the resurrection: Christ arose on the first day of the week, the day after the Sabbath. (The Sabbath was on Saturday. Only later, under Emperor Constantine in the fourth century, was the official day of rest transferred from Saturday, the seventh day, to Sunday, the first day of the week.) The first day became "the day of resurrection," and not even an atheist regime has been able to uproot this from the Russian language [*Voskresenie*, the Russian word for Sunday, means resurrection—tr]. Sunday: the first day of that new time and of that new life which shone from the tomb. And over that life, as St Paul wrote, death no longer has dominion (Rom 6:9).

Christianity began with a new experience of time, in which time ceases to be bound-up with death. "O death, where is thy sting? O hell, where is thy victory?" (1 Cor 15:55). This new experience is the very heart of Christianity and its fire: death is overthrown, death is no longer a hopeless divorce from life, for the resurrection has begun. A new day has arrived, the first day of the new creation which overcomes the limits of time and brings eternal joy and eternal life. That experience is the Christian basis for the celebration of Easter.

4

Magnify, O My Soul

"**M**agnify, O my soul..." So many festal hymns in
the Orthodox Church begin with the words of this
striking call to "Magnify, O my soul...," to extol, to
praise, to wonder. These words disclose a deep and most
beautiful truth about celebration and human nature. Celebration always has at its foundation joy in some spiritual truth, in some mystical reality which normally lies
hidden beneath the noise and cares of daily life. And
then, all at once, the wonder of that mystery suddenly
fills the soul with joy. It is like the person who goes
about his life with his head down almost all the time.
Hurrying, running to and fro, he keeps his eyes on the
ground to keep from stumbling and bruising himself, or
bumping into somebody. He is always busy, and his life
is choking on endless "to do" lists. But at some point, in
the midst of this empty mechanical living and frenetic
activity, he unexpectedly lifts his head. And suddenly
he sees the boundless deep blue of the sky, he sees
sunlight all around, he sees majestic white clouds, and
he senses that the world is having some kind of celebration that he doesn't have time to go to or take part in. He
senses that this celebration is totally unlike his normal
life, and yet he senses also that all the brightness of this

celebration and all its joy are meant for him. Faith, then, is above all a penetration into that celebration, into that other world so difficult to describe in everyday speech, yet which fills the whole heart and all of life with unexpected festal joy.

"Magnify, O my soul..." For people accustomed to sobriety, reason, and visible reality, these words probably mean nothing. Their souls never magnify anything, and so they deny even the presence of a soul. The mind exists; that can be accepted and understood. The mind is what calculates, explains, defines and organizes. Likewise the will presents no special difficulties. But the soul—what's that? The only way to explain it is this: the soul is the ability to feel and to recognize that mysterious celebration, to include oneself in its joy, to have it illumine all life, all in life that spreads gloom and weighs it down. "Magnify" is thus the very definition of soul. Those who have no understanding or feeling for religion want to explain religion somehow rationally as no more than human desire to get something or to be protected from something, to depend on something. To them, this sort of dependence is unworthy of human beings. Yet how can it be explained to them that what they have defined is defective faith, and not the essence of faith?

The essence of faith lies elsewhere. Consider for a moment one of the most beloved and popular services in the Orthodox Church, the so-called "akathist." Imagine yourself in one of the big city churches in Russia. Thousands of people stand in church for hours on end; candles burn; it's hot and stuffy. Yet over and over again, like the continuous streaming of a refreshing waterfall, you hear a single call, a single exultant refrain: "Rejoice!" "Rejoice, for joy has shone forth; rejoice, for sorrow has vanished; rejoice, for the dawn of the mystical day has arrived." Here there are no requests, no fears, no petitions, only pure rejoicing. These people are standing in the presence of something unspeakably beautiful, pure, radiant and joyful; they delight and do not tire of their delight. "Delight" is perhaps the best and simplest way to describe the very deepest and most important source of faith. The person who has no faith, who is concerned exclusively with the here and now of everyday activities, delights in nothing, rejoices in nothing, and sees nothing beyond his or her immediate earthly horizon. But faith begins with the experience of a broader awareness, so well described by Vladimir Solov'ev: "Beloved friend, do you do not perceive that all which we ourselves can see is but reflection, only shadow of what to our eyes remains unseen?" In the gospels Christ says that people will see with their eyes but never perceive (Mt 13:14), and indeed, how many, many such people there are who claim to see, who have acquired the most precise instruments for seeing everything, and yet they remain blind. They neither see nor hear the reality which calls forth that glad refrain: "Rejoice!" "Magnify, O my soul..." Of course I can try to explain why, how, and in what I believe. Thousands of theological and philosophical books have been written about faith, and indeed, there are rational and scientific principles which apply even here. But no step-by-step explanation can match the vigil on the eve of Annunciation when finally, after the service's lengthy development, a trio sings the long-awaited hymn: "With the voice of the archangel we cry to thee, O Pure One: Rejoice..." At that moment the entire world, with all its suffering and torment, with all its weariness and evil, with its jealousy, pettiness and emptiness, suddenly is purified and begins to radiate a Spring that is truly beyond this world. Is this just emotionalism, is it some kind of mental breakdown or self-hypnosis? No. Human beings have forgotten the truth about the world, about life, about human nature, about the soul's purity and its first-created purpose. But at that moment, the truth breaks through, and suddenly we know once again that it is possible to breath deeply and fill our lungs with the pure air of heaven, of spirit, of love. In that moment, and others like it, something is revealed which impels me to say with boundless conviction: yes, this is truth, this is beauty, and nothing on earth compares to it. In that moment, I know that heaven has descended to earth, and that the soul has found what it has thirsted for and sought so blindly and painfully.

We are constantly being told that in order to understand the world we need science, rational thought, mathematical calculation. We're not arguing against this. In its place, and within the limits of its capabilities, science is both wonderful and necessary. But we are here to speak as witnesses that there is another approach to understanding the world and life, or rather, that there exists another dimension to the world and life which science, as such, is powerless to comprehend. Besides being an object of scientific analysis, the world is also an object of delight and celebration, love, thanksgiving, and praise. This approach is no less real and no less necessary. Why impoverish human life by depriving it a priori of "the one thing needful" (Lk 10:42)? It is the opponents of religion who most of all hate this celebration and delight, and I suspect that this is not accidental, but quite deliberate, because the person who is capable of celebration and delight is above all, free. The person who can say "rejoice" unselfishly, out of the fulness of the heart's joy and love; the person who hears the words of that remarkable invitation and applies them to himself: "Magnify, O my soul..."; how can such a person be forced to believe the sad lies woven for years by a bureaucratic ideology? "No one will take your joy from you," Christ said (Jn 16:22).

The celebration of faith continues quietly and unseen in the midst of all the world's repression and sorrow. The soul pulsates and radiates with light, and is filled with heavenly joy. "Today spring rejoices and the new creation exults," the church sings, and nothing on earth is capable of taking away that joy or silencing that exultation. Here, in this joy, human beings find their true selves and their immortal souls. And for those who have found their souls, as Mikhail Lermontov wrote, "the sad songs of earth could never replace the sounds of heaven's mirth."

5

Longing for Freedom

All celebrations, and religious celebrations especially, begin with a feeling of freedom. Starting with freedom, celebrations at the same time also manifest, embody, and express the deep human thirst for freedom. Here I am speaking not merely of external or political freedom, or the freedom to work, but about life itself as freedom. In reality, of course, everything ties us down to one degree or another and subjects us to somebody or something. This is one of humanity's most basic experiences. Human beings are slaves to time, to their geography and environment, to their genetic inheritance, to their physical constitution, to climate, to the circumstances in which they live. Finally, they are slaves to life's unpredictable currents and to its inescapable conclusion. The longer humans live and the further they move away from childhood, the more clearly they see how hemmed-in they are on all sides. Oh, of course, within the limits of these boundaries, within the narrow plot of ground and time allotted to them, they are somehow free. But as a person's spirit becomes deeper and more sensitive, he or she sees more clearly how illusive and limited their freedom really is. Their sadness and longing for genuine freedom becomes deeper and deeper. "Living always in darkness and always in strife, how dark is the darkness, how narrow the strife," wrote one poet to describe human life. The deep truth of these words is felt by all but the most coarse and vulgar, those who live for the moment and keep themselves entertained with cheap thrills.

All human culture, art, and poetry is permeated with a sadness which seems to be the most human and authentic of emotions, and this sadness concerns precisely the sense of imprisonment and limitation in life, the mortality and fragility of everything in this world. Only in childhood are we unaware of this, which is why even the most impoverished childhood seems to be one continuous celebration. Life is seen as lighthearted and joyful, like an open window on a glorious spring morning, full of limitless possibilities. A person becomes an adult when this inner spirit of celebration shrinks, and in its place the perception grows that life is like a prison. Sadness suddenly enters in. And no matter how he tries to numb that sadness, if he is honest with himself, it never goes away. The Christian experience of faith can only be understood in relation to this sadness, for this is precisely where faith takes shape, within the depths of that primal, subtle, and exalted sadness, without which a person is not a person, but an animal. In Orthodox Christianity this sadness is known as "godly grief" (1 Cor 7:10), for if in spite of all their experience of restriction, fragility, and mortality human beings are still thirsting for something more, if they are never willing to accept imprisonment as the totality of human life, then we have to ask why. Why don't they accept it? Why are they still sad, and where does that sadness come from? No other creature on earth experiences this sadness. And yet human beings, no matter how often experience should convince them otherwise, continue to hold onto words like immortality, eternity, spirit, freedom, joy; they continue to use them as if they were words of exorcism. And art, which reflects human sadness, becomes the expression of the impossible dream of breaking through to that "something more," which earthly experience cannot even begin to imagine.

"Our hearts are restless," wrote St Augustine, "until they rest in You." Godly grief is this sadness and longing for freedom. To some degree, Christianity agrees with philosophies which assert that human beings have limited freedom and externally determined destinies. In the world as it is, of course, there is no genuine freedom, and wise is the person who admits that such freedom is a childish dream. Childhood is left behind, the celebration ends, and all that remains are the deaf walls of day-to-day reality. But Christianity claims that this freedom still exists, that celebration is possible and has already started, and that "your sorrow will be turned into joy" (Jn 16:20). For by its very presence, this sorrow testifies of God, of the world of joy, love and freedom, of the world human beings were created to inhabit, and for which, often unknown even to themselves, they have always longed. "Our hearts are restless..."

This restlessness which nothing can relieve and nothing can satisfy is, for Christians, the primary evidence of God's presence. But it is not for lack of trying that the restlessness goes unrelieved. Not a century has passed without someone's trumpeting the latest solution to all problems, to all of humanity's searching. Here's the truth! Get complete peace and satisfaction! But in reality,

nowhere did anything ever deliver this peace. Today we
still hear the claim: we've found the truth, here it is in this
theory, in this doctrine. "You'll see; a few years will go
by and then we'll have a new world, a new society, a new
system that will give human beings total happiness." But
the decades go by and all we see are ruins. Who still
believes in this dead doctrine? No one.

With no exaggeration, it can safely be said that nothing except faith, and no one except God, has ever succeeded in giving not just happiness, but a truly deep
response to humanity's persistent longing for genuine,
authentic life. God and faith have responded and continue
to do so. When someone finds God, when the inner flame
of faith is lit, then childhood's lost celebration and wholeness are simultaneously returned and restored. This is
what Christ was speaking about when he said, "Become
like children" (Mt 18:3) and "Whoever does not receive
the Kingdom of God like a child shall not enter it" (Mk
10:15). To be like children means precisely to return to
life as joy and freedom.

Look at the saints. What is so striking about them is
their joy, their complete peace in this joy, and their freedom: they have that inner freedom which comes only
from assurance and confidence in the truth they have
found. That is why the Church always celebrates. That is
why the believer's entire life is defined by a rhythm of
inner preparation, approach of feast, and feast itself. Our
sadness remains, but now it is the sadness that comes
from being unable to give ourselves wholly to freedom
and joy: We are still too bound-up with ourselves, with
triviality, with pettiness, with evil. Now, sadness leads
the way into feast and celebration instead of suppressing

it. Now, there is no evil or anything else capable of conquering and stripping away that mysterious light burning within our souls, that joy no one can take away. And in the end, it is through this joy and freedom of celebration that faith will overcome a system empty of celebration, whose prosaic, colorless ideology has nothing to offer humanity.

Part II

The Church Year

1

The Elevation of the Cross

On September 14th, for centuries, when the feast of the Elevation of the Cross was celebrated in cathedrals, the bishop would take his place in the center of the church and, surrounded by a great assembly of clergy, would majestically raise the cross high over the crowd and bless the worshippers on all four sides of the church while the choir thundered in response, "Lord have mercy!" This was the celebration of Christian empire, an empire born under the sign of the Cross on that day when Emperor Constantine saw a vision of the Cross high in the sky and heard the words "In this sign conquer..." This is the feast of Christianity's triumph over kingdoms, cultures and civilizations, the feast of that Christian world which now lies in ruins, still crumbling before our very eyes.

Yes, the solemn, ancient rite will once again be celebrated this year. The choir will still be joyfully singing that "the Cross is the strength of kings, the Cross is the beauty of the universe." But today, the tumultuous metropolis surrounding the church does not participate in that hidden triumph and is completely unconnected to it. Its millions of inhabitants will go on with their normal lives and their usual ups and downs, interests, joys, and

sorrows, with no reference whatsoever to the goings-on
within the church building. Why then do we keep repeating words about universal triumph, and singing over and
over again that the Cross is unconquerable? Sadly, we
have to admit that many, many Christians are unable to
answer this question. They are accustomed to seeing the
church in exile and on the margins of life, exiled from
culture, life, schools and from everywhere. Many Christians are content and undisturbed when the authorities
contemptuously allow them to "observe their rites" as
long as they are quiet and obedient, and do not interfere
in the building of a world where there is no Christ, no
faith, and no prayer. Those tired Christians have almost
forgotten what Christ said on the night he went to the
Cross: "In the world you have tribulation, but take courage, I have overcome the world" (Jn 16:33).

It seems to me that we continue to celebrate the
Elevation of the Cross and repeat ancient words of victory not simply to commemorate an old battle that was
won, or to recall a past that no longer exists, but in order
to reflect more deeply on the meaning of the word "victory" for Christian faith. It may be that only now, stripped
as we are of outward power and glory, government support, untold wealth, and of all apparent symbols of victory, are we capable of understanding that all of this was,
perhaps, not genuine victory. Yes, the cross raised above
the crowds was in those days covered with gold and silver
and adorned with precious stones. Yet neither gold, nor
silver, nor precious stones can erase the original meaning
of the Cross as an instrument of humiliation, torture, and
execution on which a man was nailed, a man rejected by
all, gasping from pain and thirst. Do we have the courage

to ask ourselves: if all those Christian kingdoms and cultures died, if victory was replaced by defeat, was it not because we Christians became blind to the ultimate meaning and genuine content of Christianity's most important symbol? We decided that gold and silver would be allowed to eclipse this meaning. And we decided as well that God desires our worship of the past.

To honor the Cross, to raise it up, to sing of Christ's victory: does this not mean, above all, to believe in the Crucified One and to believe that the Cross is a sign of staggering defeat? For only because it is a defeat, and only to the measure it is accepted as defeat, does the Cross become victory and triumph. No, Christ did not enter the world to win outward victories. He was offered a kingdom, but refused. And at the very moment of his betrayal to death, He said: "Do you think that I cannot appeal to my Father, and he will at once send me more than twelve legions of angels?" (Mt 26:53). Yet, Christ was never more a king than when He walked to Golgotha carrying his own cross on his shoulders while the hate-filled and mocking crowd surrounded him. His kingship and power were never more obvious than when Pilate brought him before the crowd, dressed in purple, condemned to a criminal's death, a crown of thorns on his head, and Pilate telling the raging mob: "Behold your king." Only here can the whole mystery of Christianity be seen, for Christianity's victory resides within the joyful faith that here, through this rejected, crucified and condemned man, God's love began to illumine the world and a Kingdom was opened which no one has power to shut.

Each of us, however, must accept Christ and receive him with all our heart, all our soul, and all our hope.

Otherwise, outward victories are all meaningless. Perhaps we needed this outward defeat of the Christian world. Perhaps we needed poverty and rejection to purge our faith of its earthly pride and of its trust in outward power and victory, to purify our vision of the Cross of Christ, which is raised high above us even when neither we nor the world can see it. In spite of everything, the Cross is still elevated, exalted and triumphant. "The Cross is the beauty of the universe." For in whatever darkness people find themselves, and however great the outward triumph of evil in this world, the heart still knows and hears the words, "Take courage, I have overcome the world."

2

Christmas

The Sun of Righteousness

The date of Jesus Christ's birth is not recorded in the gospels. The time of year is not even mentioned, although from the reference to shepherds "abiding in the field, keeping watch over their flocks by night" (Lk 2:8) one might conclude that his birth was in summertime. This uncertainty begs the question: how and why did Christians settle on December 25th as the date of Christmas? This is much more than a trivia question, because in answering it we also learn something crucial about Christian faith, or rather, about how Christians understand their connection to the world around them which did not yet know and believe in Christ.

To answer this question we need to know that while Christianity was first spreading through the Greco-Roman world in the first few centuries A.D., that the cult of the sun, the last of the major nature religions, was spreading simultaneously and just as quickly. In the 70's of the third century, Emperor Aurelian even designated this as the official religion of the entire Roman Empire. This religion glorified the sun as the source of life, and therefore as the highest divine power. Here, as in all natural religion, was the deification of nature, of natural life-

forces. The biggest celebration of sun worship took place
in the last days of December during the winter solstice,
when the days are the shortest and now begin to grow
longer, bringing growth in warmth and light as spring
approaches, as nature is resurrected, and as life triumphs
over winter's death. In those days, of course, people did
not know that the earth orbits around the sun. To them, the
winter solstice was the victory of light over darkness; the
resurrection of nature, a divine miracle. And at the center
of this miracle was the sun, the wellspring of light and life.

Sun worship became the last great cult, and the winter
solstice the last great festival of a religious worldview
whose death was already inevitable. And this cult, therefore, became Christianity's fiercest opponent and competition, giving Christianity its last battle for the heart and
soul of the Roman Empire.

Less than fifty years after Emperor Aurelian, at the
beginning of the fourth century, Emperor Constantine
converted from sun worship to Christianity. The persecu-
tions ended, the Christian church could now openly organ-
ize her life, build churches and, most importantly, preach
her faith without interference. Historians have calculated
that at the time of Constantine's conversion, no more than
ten percent of the Empire's population was Christian, and
of these, almost all were city-dwellers. The rural population was almost untouched by Christianity. So preaching
the message of Christ as Savior to these 90 percent and
bringing them into the new faith became Christianity's
most essential task. To do this, however, meant displacing
sun worship, not outwardly and violently, but from within,
convincing people not only of Christianity's superiority,
but of its universal and saving truth.

The chief method for attracting converts was the use of their own beliefs, transforming them, purifying them and filling them with Christian content. Followers of the cult celebrated the birth of the sun in December, so Christians chose that day to celebrate the birth of Jesus Christ, the spiritual Sun, the authentic source of genuine spiritual light. To this day, the main Christmas hymn in the Orthodox Church includes images of sun and light: "Your nativity, O Christ our God, has shone to the world the light of wisdom, and those who worshipped the stars were taught by a star to adore You, the Sun of righteousness..." As we can see, Christianity took a theme familiar to all followers of natural religion—the sun as light and life—and used it to show its own faith in Christ. In effect, the church told the world, "You believe in the sun, but this physical sun of the natural world must itself be the symbol, reflection and instrument of another, transcendent, spiritual, Divine Sun, who is the source of life, light and victory...You glorify the birth of the physical sun, and we invite you to glorify the coming of the Divine Sun into the world; we call you out of the physical and visible world and invite you to enter the spiritual and invisible world."

So the feast of Christmas became the fulfillment of the feast of the sun. It became the celebration of an event that completed and fulfilled the longings, expectations and beliefs of all people. Everything that was included in the worship of the sun—faith in the world's meaningfulness, inner light, intelligence and divinity—was now given a name: Christ. Christmas thus arose as both the crowning of all humanity's longings and its unquenchable thirst for meaning and goodness, and as the beginning of a new religious era in which worship is transferred from nature and its blind forces to the One who is above nature even while being reflected within it, and is himself the source, content and goal of all life. Natural religion—the worship of creation, not the Creator—was thus overturned from within. And by accepting Christ as "the light of wisdom," human beings were liberated from slavery to the world and to nature.

The Light of Wisdom

"Your nativity, O Christ our God, has shone to the world the light of wisdom..." The main hymn of Christmas begins by affirming that in Christ's birth, the world is given not only the image of a perfect human being, but also "the light of wisdom," the most transcendent and all-embracing revelation of meaning. The light of wisdom! Here precisely is the ancient battleground against Christianity and Christ. Arrayed in opposition are all who, in the name of wisdom, feel compelled to destroy everything in any way related to the Child from Bethlehem. Their argument with Christianity and Christ has continued for almost two-thousand years.

The apostle Paul came to the Areopagus in Athens, where all the bright lights of science and philosophy held court, and there, at antiquity's heart, he preached the crucified and resurrected Christ. These sages mocked him; and soon, it was as if all the power of the great Roman Empire joined them in mockery and offered support. For two hundred years Rome fought, persecuted, and killed Christians, labelling them expendable outlaws and pariahs. Christians were slandered, their teachings derided, their rituals ridiculed. But in the midst of this darkness and malice the same Apostle Paul writes to the

Christians with such simplicity and tranquility: "We are treated as impostors and yet are true; as unknown and yet well known; as dying and behold we live; as punished, and yet not killed; as sorrowful, yet always rejoicing; as poor, yet making many rich; as having nothing, and yet possessing everything" (2 Cor 6:8-10).

The years went by. Little by little the philosophers and scholars began to reflect on the teaching that once seemed to them so incomprehensible, irrational and peculiar. Consider for example a second-century philosopher named Justin, whose works have come down to us. His whole life had been spent in pursuit of truth; he had studied every area of knowledge, and finally he came to Christianity. What led him to this persecuted faith and to a martyr's death? His answer: "the light of wisdom." He discovered the transcendent and all- encompassing wisdom of Christian revelation. He discovered that Christianity alone was capable of answering all questions and satisfying completely the mind's seeking and the heart's thirst.

A few more decades, and we find another representative of ancient Olympus: Clement of Alexandria. With him as well, Christian faith is revealed as the height of human reason, the goal and fulfillment of all searching and hope. Christianity, he said, is meaning and wisdom itself, or "Logos." The gospels claim that Christ is the Logos, the Word who gives meaning and makes sense of everything else.

How many there were like Justin and Clement. The Empire itself finally bowed its proud head before the Crucified Teacher whom she so long disdained. Thus began the Christian era in human history and culture. Is it really possible to forget the roots which gave rise to virtually everything through which we live and breathe in western society? Christianity has entered the flesh and blood of our life, and without it we can understand neither art, nor philosophy, nor science.

Today, however, the pride of the human mind rebels once again against the treasure-house of wisdom, goodness and beauty. What holds this rebellion together? Raw power, for in the final analysis, the enemies of Christianity have no other arguments whatsoever except slander and propaganda. In answer, and with no less force, the churches ring out with a song of victory: "Your Nativity, O Christ our God, has shone to the world the light of wisdom..." With conviction equal to that of our opponents, and just as firmly, we proclaim that honest searching, thirst, and love for the truth will sooner or later lead to Christ. "For in him was life, and the life was the light of men...The light shines in the darkness, and the darkness has not overcome it" (Jn 1: 4-5). It is precisely in this affirmation, in this confession, that we find the meaning of Christmas. The light of wisdom which entered the world and began to shine within it those two thousand years ago has neither left us nor been extinguished. We have progressed so much in our study of the world in these twenty centuries, that the best minds of our time are beginning to sense God's glory and the light of His wisdom as they explore the limits of the universe, its order and its beauty. The star which led the wise men to the cave is no longer simply a touching story, as once again we hear the eternal truth of the psalm: "The heavens are telling the glory of God and the firmament proclaims his handiwork!" (Ps 19:1).

The whole world strives for unity, peace, love. But are these to be found in economics? In the arms race? In competition? It is becoming increasingly obvious that there is an ever-deepening desire for something that will truly go to the very heart of humanity, as the all-illuminating light of life. Yet the "very heart" is no other than Christ himself. And there is no other path to this heart except the path He gave in the commandment of love: "Love one another, even as I have loved you..." (Jn 13:34). And there is no other wisdom and no other goal except the Kingdom of God He proclaimed. The light of Christmas is precisely this cosmic light and love. With spiritual hearing we can still hear the very same triumphant praise of two-thousand years ago: "Glory to God in the highest and on earth peace, good will among men" (Lk 2:14). With spiritual eyesight we can see the same light of wisdom, and with spiritual voices we can respond to this joyful proclamation with the same song of thanksgiving: "Christ is born; glorify him! Christ comes from heaven; go to meet him! Christ is on earth; be uplifted!"

The Divine Child

"The eternal God was born as a little child." One of the main hymns of Christmas ends with these words, identifying the child born in a Bethlehem cave as "the eternal God." This hymn was composed in the sixth century by the famous Byzantine hymnographer Roman the Melodist:

> Today the Virgin gives birth to the Transcendent One,
> And the earth offers a cave to the Unapproachable One!
> Angels, with shepherds, glorify him!
> The wise men journey with the star!
> Since for our sake the eternal God was born as a little child! (Kontakion of Christmas)

The Child as God, God as Child...Why does joyful excitement build over the Christmas season as people, even those of lukewarm faith and unbelievers, behold that unique, incomparable sight of the young mother holding the child in her arms, and around them the "wise men from the East," the shepherds fresh from night-watch in their fields, the animals, the open sky, the star? Why are we so certain, and discover again and again, that on this sorrowful planet of ours there is nothing more beautiful and joyful than this sight, which the passage of centuries has proven incapable of uprooting from our memory? We return to this sight whenever we have nowhere else to go, whenever we have been tormented by life and are in search of something that might deliver us.

Yet in the gospel account of the birth of Jesus Christ, mother and child say not a single word, as if words were unnecessary, for no words can explain, define or express the meaning of what took place and was fulfilled that night. And nevertheless we use words here, not to explain, or to interpret, but because, as the Scriptures say, "Out of the abundance of the heart the mouth speaks" (Mt 12:34). It is impossible for someone with an overflowing heart not to share this with others.

It is the words "child" and "God" which give us the most striking revelation about the Christmas mystery. In a certain profound way, this is a mystery directed toward the child who continues to secretly live within every adult, to the child who continues to hear what the adult no longer hears, and who responds with a joy which the adult, in his mundane, grown-up, tired and cynical world, is no longer capable of feeling. Yes, Christmas is a feast for children, not just because of the tree that we decorate and light, but in the much deeper sense that children alone are unsurprised that when God comes to us on earth, he comes as a child.

This image of God as child continues to shine on us through icons and through innumerable works of art, revealing that what is most essential and joyful in Christianity is found precisely here, in this eternal childhood of God. Adults, even those most sympathetic to "religious themes," desire and expect religion to give explanations and analysis; they want it to be intelligent and serious. Its opponents are just as serious, and in the end, just as boring, as they confront religion with a hail of "rational" bullets. In our society, nothing better conveys our contempt than to say "it's childish." In other words, it's not for adults, for the intelligent and serious. So children grow up and become equally serious and boring. Yet Christ said "become like children" (Mt 18:3). What does this mean? What are adults missing, or better, what has been choked, drowned or deafened by a thick layer of adulthood? Above all, is it not that capacity, so characteristic of children, to wonder, to rejoice and, most importantly, to be whole both in joy and sorrow? Adulthood chokes as well the ability to trust, to let go and give one's self completely to love and to believe with all one's being. And finally, children take seriously what adults are no longer capable of accepting: dreams, that which breaks though our everyday experience and our cynical mistrust, that deep mystery of the world and everything within it revealed to saints, children, and poets.

Thus, only when we break through to the child living hidden within us, can we inherit as our own the joyful mystery of God coming to us as a child. The child has neither authority nor power, yet the very absence of authority reveals him to be a king; his defenselessness and vulnerability are precisely the source of his profound power. The child in that distant Bethlehem cave has no desire that we fear him; He enters our hearts not by frightening us, by proving his power and authority, but by love alone. He is given to us as a child, and only as children can we in turn love him and give ourselves to him. The world is ruled by authority and power, by fear and domination. The child God liberates us from that. All He desires from us is our love, freely given and joyful; all He desires is that we give him our heart. And we give it to a defenseless, endlessly trusting child.

Through the feast of Christmas, the Church reveals to us a joyful mystery: the mystery of freely given love imposing itself on no one. A love capable of seeing, recognizing and loving God in the Divine Child, and becoming the gift of a new life.

After Christmas

No sooner have we encountered the joy of Christmas, that celebration of peace and goodwill radiating from the Child of Bethlehem, then the gospel calls us to witness an explosion of horrific malice toward him, a malice which will never end and never weaken.

> Now when Jesus was born in Bethlehem of Judea in the days of Herod the king, behold, wise men from the East came to Jerusalem, saying, "Where is he who has been born king of the Jews? For we have seen his star in the East, and have come to worship him." When Herod the king heard this, he was troubled... and assembling all the chief priests and scribes of the people, he inquired of them where the Christ was to be born. They told him, "In Bethlehem of Judea; for so it is written by

the prophet..." Then Herod summoned the wise men secretly and ascertained from them what time the star appeared; and he sent them to Bethlehem, saying, "Go and search diligently for the child, and when you have found him bring me word, that I too may come and worship him." When they had heard the king they went their way; and lo, the star which they had seen in the East went before them, till it came to rest over the place where the child was. When they saw the star, they rejoiced exceedingly with great joy; and going into the house they saw the child with Mary his mother, and they fell down and worshipped him. Then, opening their treasures, they offered him gifts, gold, and frankincense and myrrh. And being warned in a dream not to return to Herod, they departed to their own country by another way. Now when they had departed, behold, an angel of the Lord appeared to Joseph in a dream and said, "Rise, take the child and his mother, and flee to Egypt, and remain there till I tell you; for Herod is about to search for the child to destroy him." And he arose and took the child and his mother by night, and departed to Egypt... Then Herod, when he saw that he had been tricked by the wise men, was in a furious rage, and he sent and killed all the male children in Bethlehem and in all that region who were two years old or under, according to the time which he had ascertained from the wise men. Then was fulfilled what was spoken by the prophet Jeremiah: "A voice was heard in Ramah, wailing and loud lamentation, Rachel weeping for her children; she refused to be consoled, because they were no more." (Mt 2:1-18)

Such is the gospel account. Let us leave aside some of the questions this story undoubtedly raises for modern readers: who were these wise men who came from the East to worship Christ? How do we understand the star that led them to Bethlehem? Which prophets foretold the birth of the Savior in Bethlehem? And so on. These questions have all been researched by many scholars of Holy Scripture, and while their conclusions are interesting, the most important aspect of the story is elsewhere: Herod's reaction.

Historically, we know that Herod reigned in Palestine with the consent and protection of the Roman occupiers, and that he was a cruel and unjust tyrant. In his reaction to the birth of Christ, the gospel gives us an eternal portrait of earthly authority whose sole purpose and full strength is devoted to holding, wielding and defending its power against any perceived threat to its existence. Don't we ourselves so well know this experience? Above all, Herod is fearful and suspicious. How, we might ask, could a child possibly be a threat, a child for whose very birth no place could be found except a cave? But for Herod it was enough that someone—in this case, those mysterious wise men from the East—gave the name "king" to this unknown, poor and helpless child. Nothing more was needed to set in motion the machinery of criminal investigation, search, interrogation and persecution.

"Then Herod secretly called the wise men..." It had to be in secret, for this type of authority knows it can operate only when its work is carried out in secret, and that means without law, without justice. And then, "Go," Herod tells the wise men, "and search diligently for the child." He gives the order to investigate, to "build a case," to prepare it carefully so there are no slips or blunders as the reprisal is readied. And then a lie: "Bring me word, that I too may come and worship Him." How often we have seen this kind of lie that takes shape so methodically as it prepares to strike. And finally, the insane and bloody reprisal: to destroy one, kill hundreds. Take no chances, stop at nothing. And all to protect the coveted power which has no other means of support except violence, cruelty and readiness to kill.

The light of Christmas meets the darkness of malevolent power corrupted by fear and suspicion. On one side: "Glory to God in the highest and on earth peace, goodwill among men." And on the other side, a terrifying, perpetual bad will, the dying breath of a dead regime which hates light, the world, freedom, love, and desires to utterly uproot them with no pity whatsoever. What do these authorities care about the crying and weeping of mothers who cannot and will not be comforted? Two-thousand years have passed since that time, but the same two forces continue to face each other on our long-suffering planet: the authority of naked power, blind in its fear and terrifying in its cruelty; and the radiant authority of Bethlehem's child. It may seem that all power, all might, is in the hands of that earthly authority, its police, its interrogators, its immortal cadre of late-night operatives. But only apparently: for the star, and the image of Mother and Child never stop shining; the song is not silenced, "Glory to God in the highest"; and faith, hope and love live on. Christmas has come and gone, but its radiance remains.

3

The New Year

It's an old custom: on New Year's Eve, while the clock strikes midnight, we think of our aspirations for the new year and try to enter the unknown future with a dream, looking forward to the fulfillment of some cherished desire. Today we once again are approaching a new year. What do we desire for ourselves, for others, for everyone? What is the goal of all our hopes? The answer is always the same eternal word: happiness. Happy New Year! New happiness for a New Year! The particular happiness we desire is of course different and personal for each of us, but we all share in common the faith that this year, happiness might be around the corner, that we can look forward and hope for it.

But when is a person genuinely happy? After centuries of experience and everything we have learned about human beings, we can no longer equate happiness with externals of any kind—money, health, or success, for example. We know that none of these corresponds completely to that mysterious and ever elusive notion of happiness. Clearly, physical comfort brings happiness, but not completly. Money brings happiness, but also anxiety. Success brings happiness, but also fear. It is striking that the more external happiness we have, the more fragile it becomes and the more intractable the fear that we will lose it and be left empty-handed. Perhaps this is why we wish each other new happiness in the New Year. The "old" happiness never materialized, something was always missing. But now once again we look ahead with a prayer, a dream, a hope...

My goodness! The gospel long ago recorded the story of a man who became rich, built new barns to store his grain, and decided he now had everything necessary to guarantee his happiness! He was comfortable and at ease. But that night he was told: "Fool! This night your soul is required of you; and the things you have prepared, whose will they be?" (Lk 12:20). The gradual realization that nothing can be held onto, that ahead of us lies inevitable death and decay, is the venom which poisons the little and limited happiness that we do have. This is surely why we have the custom of making such a din of noise-makers, shouting, and loud laughter as the clock strikes midnight on New Year's Eve. We are afraid of being alone and in silence when the clock strikes as the merciless voice of fate: one strike, a second, a third, and so on, so inexorably, so evenly, so terribly, to the end. Nothing can change it, nothing can stop it.

Thus we have two truly deep and indestructible poles of human consciousness: fear and happiness, nightmare and dream. The new happiness we dream about on New Year's Eve would finally be able to calm, disperse and conquer fear; we dream of a happiness which has no fear lurking deep within, a fear from which we are always trying to protect ourselves, by drinking, by keeping busy, by surrounding ourselves with noise. Yet the silence of that fear is still louder than any noise. "Fool!" Yes, the immortal dream of happiness is by nature foolish in a world infected by fear and death. And at the highest points of human culture, people are well-aware of this. One can feel the grief and sad truth behind the words of the great and life-loving poet Aleksandr Pushkin when he wrote: "In the world there is no happiness." Indeed, a profound grief permeates all genuine art. Only down below, at the bottom of human culture, do crowds go wild with noise and shouting, as if noise and feverish partying could bring happiness.

"In Him was life, and the life was the light of men. The light shines in the darkness, and the darkness has not overcome it" (Jn 1:4-5). What this means is that the light cannot be swallowed-up by fear and anxiety, it cannot be dispersed by sadness and hopelessness. In this vain thirst for momentary happiness, if only people would find within themselves the strength to stop, to think, to look at the depth of life! If only they would listen to the words, to the voice calling to them eternally within those depths. If only they knew what genuine happiness truly is. "And no one will take your joy from you" (Jn 16:22). Isn't this what we dream about when the clock strikes midnight: joy that cannot be taken away? But how rarely we reach such depth! How we fear it for some reason, and put it aside: "Not today, but tomorrow, or the day after, I'll turn my attention to what's essential and eternal; only, not today. There's still time."

But there is really so little time. Only moments go by before the arrow of time whizzes to its fateful target. Why delay? For right here, in our very midst, Someone stands beside us: "Behold, I stand at the door and knock" (Rev 3:20). If we would only set aside our fear and look at

Him, we would see such light, such joy, and such abundance of life that we would surely understand the meaning of that elusive and mysterious word "happiness."

4

The Lord's Baptism

Water

Water doesn't mean much to us today. It's one of life's essential comforts, accessible, automatic, cheap. You turn on the tap and there it is... However, for thousands of years water was a primary religious symbol, and to understand why this was so we must recover the almost completely extinguished feeling for the cosmos.

To people of the ancient world, water was no less than the symbol of life itself, and of the world as life...Water is truly a precondition for life. One can go without food for a long time, but without water a person will die very quickly, so we can say that human beings are by nature thirsty beings. Without water, cleanliness is impossible, so water is also the symbol of cleansing and purity. Water as life and as purity, but also beauty, power and might, as we see it reflect and absorb, so to speak, the boundless blue sky. All of this describes the perception or experience of water that placed it at the center of religious symbolism.

Go into a church on the eve of Epiphany while the "Great Blessing of Water" is being celebrated. Listen to the words of the prayers and hymns, pay attention to the rite, and you will feel that there is more here than merely

ancient ritual: it has something to say to us today, just as
it did a thousand years ago, about our life and our perpetual and unquenchable thirst for purification, rebirth, renewal... In this celebration water becomes what it was on
the first day of Creation, when "the earth was without
form and void, and darkness was upon the face of the
deep; and the Spirit of God was moving over the face of
the waters " (Gen 1:2). The words of the service echo this
in praise and thanksgiving: "Great are You, O Lord, and
marvellous are Your works, and there are no words which
suffice to hymn Your wonders..." Once again, a beginning. Once again, humanity stands before the mystery of
existence. Once again, we experience the world joyfully
and we see its beauty and harmony as God's gift. Once
again, we give thanks. And in this thanksgiving, praise,
and joy, we once again become genuine human beings.

The joy of Epiphany is in the recovery of a cosmic
experience of the world, of recovering faith that everything and everyone can always be washed, purified, renewed, reborn, and that regardless how dirty and clouded
with mud our life has become, no matter what swamp we
might have rolled in, we always have access to a purifying stream of living water, because humanity's thirst for
heaven, goodness, perfection and beauty is not dead, nor
can it ever die. Indeed, this thirst alone makes us human
beings. "Great art You, O Lord, and marvellous are Your
works, and there are no words which suffice to hymn
Your wonders..." Who said that Christianity is depressing
and grim, morbid and sad, and pulls human beings away
from life? Look at the faces of worshippers that night, and
see the light and joy that shines as they listen to the psalm
thundering its exultation, "The voice of the Lord is upon

the waters" (Ps 29:3), as they watch the priest sprinkling volleys of blessed water throughout the church, and those glittering drops fly as if throughout the whole world, making that world once again a possibility and a promise, the raw material for a mysterious miracle of transformation and transfiguration. God himself entered this water in the form of a man; He united himself not only with humanity, but with all matter, and made all of it a radiant, lightbearing stream flowing toward life and joy.

But none of this can be experienced or sensed without repentance, without a deep change of consciousness, without the conversion of mind and heart, without the ability to see everything in a new light. This was precisely the repentance John the Baptist preached and which made it possible to see Jesus approaching the river Jordan, and lovingly accept him as God himself, who from the beginning of time loved the human race and created the whole world for us as an image of his love, eternity and joy.

Jesus at the Jordan

The evangelist Mark describes the baptism of Christ in the following words:

> John the Baptizer appeared in the wilderness, preaching a baptism of repentance for the forgiveness of sins. And there went out to him all the country of Judea, and all the people of Jerusalem; and they were baptized by him in the river Jordan, confessing their sins. Now John was clothed in camel's hair, and had a leather girdle around his waist, and ate locusts and wild honey. And he preached, saying, "After me comes he who is mightier than I, the thong of whose sandals I am not worthy to stoop down and untie. I have baptized you with water; but he will baptize you with the Holy

Spirit." In those days Jesus came from Nazareth of Galilee and was baptized by John in the Jordan. And when he came up out of the water, immediately he saw the heavens opened and the Spirit descending upon him like a dove; and a voice came from heaven, "You are my beloved Son; with You I am well pleased." (Mk 1:4-11)

As we can see, John not only called people to repentance, he also claimed that his teaching was preparing the way for someone else more mighty, One who would baptize not merely with water, but with the Holy Spirit. When this "someone mightier," as John called him, came to the Jordan to be baptized himself by John, the moment was accompanied by mysterious events confirming the truth of John's prophecy, as if to say "yes, this is the very one whose coming I announced to you." This short gospel story pulls together many themes or strands and weaves them together into a unified whole.

The first theme is John and his preaching of repentance and baptism. John belongs to that order of spiritual people whose vocation is to reveal to a particular society at a particular moment in history the injustice, lies and evil which feed and poison that society. His mission is to provoke a spiritual and moral crisis that forces people to examine the evil, to be horrified, and therefore to desire liberation. Baptism is precisely a sign of liberation, of a fundamental change of life, as the person is immersed in water, which is both the symbol of life, the fountain of life and the symbol of cleansing and regenerative power. We can conclude therefore from the gospel account that Christ's appearance and the start of his preaching coincided with a spiritual and moral crisis in society, a crisis that was inciting repentance and thirst for renewal.

Bound up with this moral crisis was the expectation of some sort of decisive event, the coming of someone who would fulfil and complete John's work, transforming his baptism into mystical baptism by the Holy Spirit. Expectancy, then, is the second strand that runs through the gospel story, and we know from the other evangelists that its focus was the coming of the Christ, i.e., of the Savior promised by God and foretold by the Old Testament prophets. St Luke, for example, speaks directly about this: "The people were in expectation, and all men questioned in their hearts concerning John, whether perhaps he were the Christ..." (Lk 3:15). Thus, the coming of Jesus Christ to John at the Jordan was the appearance of the One Promised and Foretold, the completion and fulfillment of all the prophecies concerning the Savior. A third evangelist, St Matthew, testifies to this fulfillment: "John would have prevented him, saying, 'I need to be baptized by you, and do you come to me?' But Jesus answered him, 'Let it be so now; for thus it is fitting for us to fulfil all righteousness...'" (Mt 3: 14-15).

The third strand is Christ's own baptism, his immersion in the waters of the Jordan by John. But if He is the Savior, why does He need to be baptized? Isn't baptism a symbol of repentance and purification? Yet when John expresses these doubts, Jesus answers by firmly demanding baptism, and John complies. For centuries now, the Church has been reflecting on this descent, this self-emptying of the one whom she recognizes as Savior and God, reflecting on the meaning of his condescension for the world, for the human race, for each of us.

The fourth and last strand begins right after the baptism, with the obscure, metaphorical description of a

dove mysteriously appearing and descending upon Christ
as He comes out of the water, the voice from heaven, and
these words: "And behold, the heavens were opened to
him" (Mt 3:16).

As we can see, not one but at least four themes, four
dimensions of the gospel event are united in this joyful
feast of the Lord's Baptism. And all of these we will
examine more closely in the next talk.

"He took our infirmity"

Why did Jesus, the Son of God, who came into the
world to heal sin by his own sinlessness and to bring
human beings into communion with divine life, desire,
and indeed demand, to be baptized by John? We know
from the gospel that this question was also at the center
of John's heart. "I need to be baptized by you, and you
come to me?" (Mt 3:14). The following is the Church's
response.

By accepting baptism, Christ identifies himself with
all people, with all sinners without exception. He identifies himself with every sinner in need of forgiveness,
salvation and rebirth... He identifies himself with all and
with each one of us. In being baptized, He demonstrates
that He came not to judge or condemn, not to bring rules
and laws from outside, so to speak, from on high, from
the heights of his perfection and divinity, but to be united
with us, so that in becoming one of us, He might make us
partakers of his perfect and sinless life. John the Baptist
said of him, "Behold, the Lamb of God, who takes away
the sin of the world!" (Jn 1:29). Christ entered our world
as a child, and in his birth He took upon himself, and
made his own, our human nature. The Son of God became

the Son of Man. And He did this not for the righteous, but for sinners, for the lost. He loves them with sacrificial love, He gives himself and his whole life to them. Here, in John's baptism, He, the Sinless One, joins with us sinners; He, the Savior, joins with the lost, for there is no sin which can overcome God's love for us. In being baptized He unites himself with the life of sinful human beings, just as later on, at the end He, the Deathless One, also freely unites himself with human beings in death. All of this testifies that Christ desires to save us through love; and only through love, but love means, above all, union with the one whom you love. As the prophet Isaiah said, "He took our infirmities and bore our diseases...and with his wounds we are healed" (Is 53:4, 5).

There is however a second and still deeper, more joyful meaning in the Baptism of our Lord and Savior in the waters of the Jordan. After the Epiphany service, the faithful leave the church and go outdoors to bless water. The triumphant, exultant words of the psalm ring out: "The voice of the Lord is upon the waters" (Ps 29:3), and we are shown the meaning and significance of water as the image of life, as the image of the world and all creation. And the one who descends into the water, who is immersed in the water, who unites himself with it by coming into the world for its salvation and rebirth—that One is God. The world tore away from God, forgot him, stopped seeing him and immersed itself in sin, darkness and death. But God did not forget the world. Here, in his baptism, God returns it to us, shining with the glory of the stars and the beauty it had on the first day of creation. "If anyone thirsts, let him come to me and drink. He who believes in me...out of his heart shall flow rivers of living water" (Jn 7:37, 38). Everything in this world, including matter itself, its very substance, now once again becomes a path toward God, toward communion with him, toward growth in this abundant and eternal life. What we celebrate on this joyful and radiant day of Epiphany is the coming of God to his own creation. "And behold, the heavens were opened to him" (Mt 3:16). We don't know what exactly John felt when his hands touched the Savior, or how he saw the heavens opened, or how he heard the voice. But that moment was for him undoubtedly one of blinding light, when everything ignited and burst into flame with the joy of creations's first beauty, as the world once again was revealed as God's world, purified, washed, reborn, filled with praise and thanksgiving.

"Christ has come to renew all creation." We celebrate renewal when we see the priest sprinkling the church, us, our homes, all nature and all the world with new, holy, and divine water; and when we see people streaming forward to partake of that living water which flows into eternal life. And so, let everyone who thirsts come to him and receive the gift of living water, the gift of new life, pure and reborn.

5

The Meeting of the Lord*

Forty days after Christmas, parishes of the Orthodox Church celebrate the Meeting of the Lord. Since it usually falls on a weekday, this feast is half-forgotten, but nonetheless this is when the Church completes "the time of Christmas," revealing and recapitulating the full meaning of Christmas in a stream of pure and profound joy. The feast commemorates and contemplates an event recorded in the gospel of Saint Luke. Forty days after the birth of Jesus Christ in Bethlehem, Joseph and Mary, keeping to the religious practice of that time, "brought the child to Jerusalem, to present him to the Lord as it is written in the law of the Lord..." (Lk 2:22, 23). The gospel continues,

> Now there was a man in Jerusalem, whose name was Simeon, and this man was righteous and devout...and the Holy Spirit was upon him. And it had been revealed to him by the Holy Spirit that he should not see death before he had seen the Lord's Christ. And inspired by the Spirit he came into the temple; and when the parents brought in the child Jesus, to do for him according to the custom of the law, he took him up in his arms and blessed God and

*Fr. Alexander wrote this sermon just two weeks before his death.

71

said, "Lord, now lettest thou thy servant depart in peace,
according to thy word; for mine eyes have seen thy
salvation which thou hast prepared in the presence of all
peoples, a light for revelation to the Gentiles, and for
glory to thy people Israel." And his father and his
mother marvelled at what was said about him; and
Simeon blessed them and said to Mary his mother, "Behold, this child is set for the fall and rising of many in
Israel, and for a sign that is spoken against (and a sword
shall pierce through your own soul also), that thoughts
out of many hearts may be revealed." (Lk 2:26-35)

How striking and beautiful an image, the old man
holding the child in his arms, and how strange are his
words: "For my eyes have seen thy salvation..." Ponder-
ing these words we begin to appreciate the depth of this
event and its relationship to us, to me, to our faith. Is
anything in the world more joyful than an encounter, a
"meeting" with someone you love? Truly, to live is to
await, to look forward to the encounter. Isn't Simeon's
transcendent and beautiful anticipation a symbol of this?
Isn't his long life a symbol of expectation, this elderly
man who spends his whole life waiting for the light which
illumines all and the joy which fills everything with itself? And how unexpected, how unspeakably good that
the long-awaited light and joy comes to the elderly
Simeon through a child! Imagine the old man's trembling
hands as he takes in his arms the forty-day-old infant so
tenderly and carefully, his eyes gazing on the tiny being
and filling with an outpouring of praise: "Now, You may
let me depart in peace, for I have seen, I have held in my
arms, I have embraced the very meaning of life." Simeon
waited. He waited his entire long life, and surely this
means he pondered, he prayed, he deepened as he waited,

so that in the end his whole life was one continuous "eve" of a joyful meeting.

Isn't it time that we ask ourselves, what am I waiting for? What does my heart keep reminding me about more and more insistently? Is this life of mine gradually being transformed into anticipation, as I look forward to encountering the essential? These are the questions the Meeting poses. Here, in this feast, human life is revealed as the surpassing beauty of a maturing soul, increasingly liberated, deepened and cleansed of all that is petty, meaningless and incidental. Even aging and demise, the earthly destiny we all share, are so simply and convincingly shown here to be growth and ascent toward that one moment when with all my heart, in the fulness of thanksgiving, I say: "let me now depart." I have seen the light which permeates the world. I have seen the Child, who brings the world so much divine love and who gives himself to me. Nothing is feared, nothing is unknown, all is now peace, thanksgiving and love. This is what the Meeting of the Lord brings. It celebrates the soul meeting Love, meeting the one who gave me life and gave me strength to transfigure it into anticipation.

6

Zacchaeus

To prepare us for Great Lent, the Orthodox Church starts announcing its approach a full month before it actually begins. How difficult it is for a person to understand that besides devotion to life's other innumerable preoccupations, there is also care for the soul, for our inner world. If we were a bit more serious, we would see just how important, essential and fundamental care of the soul really is. We would then understand the slow and mysterious rhythm of church life. We know, of course, the meaning food has in our life. Some foods are good and nutritious, others are unhealthy; this one's too heavy, be careful of that one. We take great pains to ensure that the food we eat is good for us. And it is far more than pious rhetoric when we say that the soul also needs to be fed, that "man shall not live by bread alone" (Mt 4:4). Each of us knows we need time for reading, for thinking, for conversation, for leisure. Yet even to these we give very little genuine care, attention, or even the most basic hygiene. We look for light reading, for banter but not conversation, for amusement but not nourishment. We don't understand that the soul gets constipated much more easily than our digestive system, and that the consequences of a constipated soul are much more harmful. So much time is devoted to externals, and so little to the inner life. But we are now approaching that time of year when the Church calls us to remember the existence of that inner person and to be horrified by our forgetfulness, by the meaningless nonsense in which we are immersed, by the waste of precious time given to us so sparingly, by the unkempt and petty confusion in which we live.

Lent is a time of repentance, and repentance is a re-examination, a re-appraisal, a deepening, a shaking upside down. Repentance is the sorrowful uncovering of one's neglected, forgotten, soiled "inner" person. The first announcement of Lent, the first reminder, comes through a short gospel story about an entirely unremarkable man, "small of stature," whose occupation as a tax collector marked him, in that time and society, as greedy, cruel and dishonest.

Jesus entered Jericho and was passing through. And there was a man named Zacchaeus; he was a chief tax collector, and rich. And he sought to see who Jesus was, but could not, on account of the crowd, because he was small of stature. So he ran on ahead and climbed up into a sycamore tree to see him, for he was to pass that way. And when Jesus came to the place, he looked up and said to him, "Zacchaeus, make haste and come down; for I must stay at your house today." So he made haste and came down, and received him joyfully. And when they saw it they all murmured, "He has gone in to be the guest of a man who is a sinner." And Zacchaeus stood and said to the Lord, "Behold, Lord, the half of my goods I give to the poor; and if I have defrauded any one of anything, I restore it fourfold." And Jesus said to him, "Today, salvation has come to this house, since he also

is a son of Abraham. For the Son of man came to seek
and to save the lost. (Lk 19:1-10)

Zacchaeus wanted to see Christ; he wanted this so
much that his desire attracted the attention of Jesus. Desire is the beginning of everything. As the gospel says,
"Where your treasure is, there will your heart be also"
(Mt 6:21). Everything in our life begins with desire, since
what we desire is also what we love, what draws us from
within, what we surrender to. We know that Zacchaeus
loved money, and by his own admission we know that to
get it he had no scruples about defrauding others. Zacchaeus was rich and he loved riches, but within himself
he discovered another desire, he wanted something else,
and this desire became the pivotal moment of his life.

This gospel story poses a question to each of us: what
do you love, what do you desire—not superficially, but
deeply? There is no mysterious teacher walking through
your town, down your street, surrounded by crowds of
people. But is that really so? Isn't there some mysterious
calling walking by your life every moment; and somewhere in the depths of your soul, don't you sometimes
feel a longing for something other than what now fills
your life from morning till night? Stop for moment, pay
attention, enter your heart, listen to your own inner person, and you will find within yourself the very same
strange and wonderful desire Zacchaeus encountered,
which no human being can live without, yet which almost
everyone fears and suppresses with the noise and vanity
of everything external. "Behold, I stand at the door and
knock," the New Testament says (Rev 3:20). Do you hear
this quiet knock? This is the first invitation of the Church,
of the gospel, and of Christ: desire something other, take

a deep breath of something other, remember something other. And the very moment we stop to listen to that call is as if a pure and joyful wind blows into the stale air of our joyless lives, and the slow return begins.

Desire. The soul taking a deep breath. Everything becomes—has already become—different, new, boundlessly meaningful. The little man, with his eyes to the ground focusing on earthly desires, now ceases to be little as his victory over himself begins. Here is the start, the first step from exterior to interior, toward that mysterious homeland which all human beings, unknown often to themselves, long for and desire.

7

The Publican and the Pharisee

One of the main distinctive features of the gospels, and quite unique to them, are the short stories known as parables which Jesus used in his teaching and meetings with people. What is most striking is that these parables, told two thousand years ago in conditions utterly unlike our own, in a different civilization, in an absolutely different language, remain up-to-date and right on target, going straight to our heart. Other books and words written only recently, perhaps yesterday or the day before, are already old news, forgotten, vanished into oblivion. Already they don't speak to us, they're dead. But these parables, so apparently simple and unsophisticated, continue full of life. We listen to them and something happens to us, as if someone were looking straight into the deepest part of our life and telling us something just about ourselves, just about me.

In this parable of the Publican and the Pharisee we have a story about two men. The Publican was a tax-collector, an occupation universally despised in the ancient world. The Pharisee belonged to the ruling party, the elite of that society and government. In contemporary language we could say that the parable of the Publican and the Pharisee is a symbolic story about a respected representative of the ruling class, on the one hand, and a petty, disreputable "apparatchik" on the other. Christ says:

> Two men went up into the temple to pray, one a Pharisee, and the other a tax collector. The pharisee stood and prayed thus within himself, "God, I thank thee that I am not like other men, extortioners, unjust, adulterers, or even like this tax collector. I fast twice a week, I give tithes of all that I get." But the tax collector, standing far off, would not even lift up his eyes to heaven, but beat his breast, saying, "God, be merciful to me, a sinner!" I tell you, this man went down to his house justified rather than the other; for every one who exalts himself will be humbled, but he who humbles himself will be exalted. (Lk 18:10-14)

The story takes up only five short verses in the gospel, yet it contains something eternal that applies to all times and situations. For now, however, let's consider the parable only in light of our own time and ourselves. If anything lies at the foundation of our government, society, and yes, our personal lives, then it is the Pharisee's continuous self-promotion, self-affirmation, or to use a more venerable and eternal word, pride. Listening to the heartbeat of our times, we can't but be amazed at the frightening self-advertisement, boasting and shameless self-praise that has entered our life so completely that we almost don't notice it. All self-criticism, self-examination, self-assessment, and any hint of humility have become not simply weaknesses, but worse, a social or even a government crime. Loving one's country now means forever praising it brazenly while belittling other nations. Loyalty now means forever proclaiming the sinlessness of authorities. To be human now means to demean and trample others, raising yourself up by putting others

down. Analyzing your life and the life of your society, its
basic structure, you will surely admit that this is an accurate description. The world in which we live is so permeated with deafening boastfulness, it has become so
natural a part of living, that we ourselves don't even
notice it. This indeed was Boris Pasternak's observation,
as one of the greatest and most clear-sighted poets of our
time: "...everything is drowning in phariseeism..." Most
frightening, of course, is that phariseeism is accepted as
virtue. We have been inundated so long and so persist-
ently with glory, accomplishments, triumphs; we have so
long been held captive in an atmosphere of illusory
pseudo-greatness, that all this now seems good and right.
Imprinted on the soul of whole generations is now an
image of the world in which power, pride and shameless
self-praise are the norm. It is time to be horrified by all
this and to remember the words of the gospel: "Every one
who exalts himself will be humbled."

At present, those few who are just beginning to talk
about this, in a whisper, who little by little remind the
world of this, are shunted off to court or imprisoned in
psychiatric hospitals. They are hounded without pity:
"Look at these traitors! They oppose the greatness and
might of their country! They are against its accomplishments! They have doubts that we are the best, most powerful, most free, most happy country of all. Be thankful
that you are not like these unfortunate renegades." And so
on... But understand that the argument, the war being
waged by this embattled minority, is a fight for the spiritual foundations of our very life, because the Pharisee's
pride is not merely words. Sooner or later his pride fills
with hatred and turns on those who refuse to acknowledge

his greatness, his perfection. It turns on them with persecution and terror. It leads to death. Christ's parable is like a scalpel lancing the worst pus-filled boil of the contemporary world: the pride of the pharisee. For as long as this boil grows, the world will be ruled by hatred, fear and blood. And that is the situation today.

Only in returning to the forgotten, discredited, and discarded power of humility will the world be made clean. For humility means acceptance and respect of the other, the courage to admit one's own imperfection, to repent, and to set out on the path toward correction. To leave the boasting, lies and darkness of the Pharisee, and to return to the light and wholeness of genuine humanity. To turn toward truth, toward humility, and toward love. This is the call of Christ's parable, and this is the invitation, the first invitation of the lenten spring...

8

The Parable of the Prodigal Son

Here is another of Christ's parables from the gospel of Luke.

There was a man who had two sons; and the younger of them said to his father, "Father, give me the share of the property that falls to me." And he divided his living between them. Not many days later, the younger son gathered all he had and took his journey into a far country, and there he squandered his property in loose living. And when he had spent everything, a great famine arose in that country, and he began to be in want. So he went and joined himself to one of the citizens of that country, who sent him into the fields to feed swine. And he gladly would have fed on the pods that the swine ate; and no one gave him anything. But when he came to himself he said, "How many of my father's hired servants have bread enough and to spare, but I perish here with hunger! I will arise and go to my father, and I will say to him, 'Father, I have sinned against heaven and before you; I am no longer worthy to be called your son; treat me as one of your hired servants.'" And he arose and came to his father. But while he was yet at a distance, his father saw him and had compassion, and ran and embraced him and kissed him. And the son said to him, "Father, I have sinned against heaven and before you; I am no longer worthy to be called your son." But the father said to his servants, "Bring quickly the best robe, and put it on him; and put a ring on his hand, and shoes on his feet; and bring the fatted calf and kill it, and let us eat and make merry; for this my son was dead, and is alive again; he was lost, and is found." And they began to make merry.

Now his elder son was in the field; and as he came and drew near to the house, he heard music and dancing. And he called one of the servants and asked what this meant. And he said to him. "Your brother has come, and your father has killed the fatted calf, because he has received him safe and sound." But he was angry and refused to go in. His father came out and entreated him, but he answered his father, "Lo, these many years I have served you, and I never disobeyed your command; yet you never gave me a kid, that I might make merry with my friends. But when this son of yours came, who has devoured your living with harlots, you killed for him the fatted calf!" And he said to him, "Son, you are always with me, and all that is mine is yours. It was fitting to make merry and be glad, for this your brother was dead, and is alive; he was lost, and is found." (Lk 15:11-32)

This parable is read in church as believers are beginning to prepare themselves for Great Lent, the time of repentance. And perhaps nowhere else in the gospels is the essence of repentance better revealed. The prodigal son left home and went into "a far country," and it is this "far country," this foreign land which shows us the deepest essence also of our own life, of our own condition. Only if we have understood this can we begin the return to authentic life. The person who has never felt this distance, even once in his life, who has never felt himself to be in a spiritual wasteland, separated, exiled, can never understand the meaning of Christianity.

A person who is totally "at home" in this world, who has never experienced longing for a different reality, cannot comprehend remorse and repentance. These are not simply the formal enumeration of one's shortcomings, mistakes and even crimes. No, remorse and repentance are born from an experience of alienation from God and from joy in communion with him. It is relatively easy to admit my mistakes and shortcomings, but how much more difficult it is suddenly to realize that I have broken, betrayed and lost my spiritual beauty, that I am such a long way from my true home, from my true life; that something in the very fabric of my own life, something priceless, pure and beautiful has been destroyed and torn apart. But this realization is precisely repentance, and therefore necessarily involves a deep desire to go back, to return, once again to find the lost home.

All at once I begin to perceive that my heavenly Father has given me a treasure-chest of priceless gifts: first, life itself and the possibility of genuinely enjoying it, which means that I can transform it into meaning, love, knowledge. And secondly, He has given me a new life through his Son Jesus Christ; He has shown me his eternal Kingdom, joy and peace in the Holy Spirit. I was given the knowledge of God and in this knowledge I was given power to become a free and loving child of God. I lost all of this, I repudiated all of this, not only through particular "sins" and "transgressions," but through the sin of sins: by going away into a "far country," by choosing a foreign land, separation, withdrawal...

But the prodigal son remembered. He remembered the Father, the Father's house, and the lost joy of life. He arose and returned, and the Father accepted and forgave him. During these preparatory Sundays before Lent we sing in church the verses of Psalm 137: "By the waters of Babylon we sat down and wept, when we remembered Zion..." We sing this song of exile and alienation, but also of repentance, love and return. If we would only break through the pettiness of life to the memory of heart and soul which recognizes that this is not our real life, that this is not how we really live. Through a mysterious and hidden memory, heart and soul know and remember the lost home of the Father and the lost joy of life.

"I will arise and go..." How simple and how difficult. But it is upon these words alone that everything else depends, both in my own life and in the life of the world around me. Everything depends on authentic repentance, on this illumination of mind, heart and soul recognizing at once both the darkness, bitterness and sorrow of our fallen life, and the light of divine love, waiting to fill that life at any moment.

9

The Parable of the Last Judgment

Christ said,
When the Son of Man comes in his glory, and all the angels with him, then he will sit on his glorious throne. Before him will be gathered all the nations, and he will separate them one from another as a shepherd separates the sheep from the goats, and he will place the sheep at his right hand, but the goats at the left. Then the King will say to those at his right hand, "Come, O blessed of my Father, inherit the kingdom prepared for you from the foundation of the world; for I was hungry and you gave me food, I was thirsty and you gave me drink, I was a stranger and you welcomed me, I was naked and you clothed me, I was sick and you visited me, I was in prison and you came to me." Then the righteous will answer him, "Lord, when did we see thee hungry and feed thee, or thirsty and give thee drink? And when did we see thee a stranger and welcome thee, or naked and clothe thee? And when did we see thee sick or in prison and visit thee?" And the King will answer them, "Truly, I say to you, as you did it to one of the least of these my brethren, you did it to me." Then he will say to those at his left hand, "Depart from me, you cursed, into the eternal fire prepared for the devil and his angels; for I was hungry and you gave me no food, I was thirsty and you gave me no drink, I was a stranger and you did not

welcome me, naked and you did not clothe me, sick and
in prison and you did not visit me." Then they also will
answer, "Lord, when did we see thee hungry or thirsty
or a stranger or naked, or sick or in prison, and did not
minister to thee?" Then he will answer them, "Truly, I
say to you, as you did it not to one of the least of these,
you did it not to me." And they will go away into eternal
punishment, but the righteous into eternal life. (Mt
25:31-46)

The "Parable of the Last Judgment," as this passage
has been known since ancient times, is read a week before
the start of Great Lent, during which the Church calls us
to examine ourselves, our conscience, and our life against
the all the fullness of the Christian gospel, i.e., Christ's
teaching, and to return as much as possible to what is
most important, to the very heart of this teaching. Many
people often find religion's most important aspect to be
the rituals and customs, the beauty of services, the possibility of encountering the sacred, heavenly and divine.
But Christ's parable of the last judgment reveals that all
of this, if it is not based on love and directed toward love,
makes religion fruitless, needless, empty and dead.

In the end, Love will be our judge. No, not abstract
love for humanity in general, but rather love toward a
living and concrete human being. Today, Christian love
has been horribly perverted by a society which, in the
name of love for abstract humanity, calls us not to love,
but to persecute other people, whom we are commanded
to consider enemies, toward whom even pity and compassion become crimes. But in his parable of the last judgment Christ says in effect, "Dreams of happiness for
abstract humanity not only will remain dreams, but will
turn into nightmares of hatred and cruelty if our love and

care are not first addressed to individual human persons—not theoretically, but in the most concrete way possible." Christ says, "I was in prison, I was hungry, I was thirsty, I was sick." What else can this mean, but that Christ once and for all identifies himself with each human being; and Christian love, therefore, is by definition the "impossible possibility" of seeing, of recognizing, of encountering Christ in each person. We are not commanded to question and analyze whether that person is worthy of our help or has earned our concern. We are not told to find out why they are in prison or hungry or naked. We are simply told to go to them with love—and only with love, never questioning merit, worthiness, views and opinions—to encounter a human being sent by God into our life, my life...

Again and again we come to recognize that the most essential, joyful mystery of Christianity is the mystery of the person, of what makes each human being valuable to God, of what we can and must love in him or her. It is precisely this mystery which the world and its ruling ideologies have repudiated. To them, a human being is defined by externals: class, race, nationality, utilitarian value, what he or she gives to the country or, on the contrary, their mistakes and crimes. Our people vs. strangers, allies vs. enemies, us vs. them... Yet it seems that everyone is talking about liberation for human society, happiness for the world, prescriptions for humanity, the struggle for a bright, happy and liberated life. But in reality, all are united against someone else and everything is exclusively motivated by fear, suspicion and hatred. And it will be this way until people understand that to love humanity in general, to serve humanity in general, is not only a deception; it is also impossible if this love is not rooted in love for the person, for each person, a love which goes beyond any of our earthly, "human, all too human" standards and categories which we use to classify and evaluate people.

All of this has been judged once and for all by him who said, and continues to say, on behalf of each person: "I was in prison..." This I is enough for us to know that each person is a brother or sister, that each person is the object of God's revelation and love, and that each person is given to me as the possibility of fulfilling my very self through divine, life-renewing and redeeming love.

10

Forgiveness Sunday

The last day before Great Lent has always been popularly known as "Forgiveness Sunday." On that day these words of Christ are read, "If you do not forgive men their trespasses, neither will your Father forgive your trespasses" (Mt 6:15). In church that evening, each person asks forgiveness of everyone else in the "rite of forgiveness," so that we enter Lent, the time of cleansing, deepening and sanctifying our life, reconciled with one another.

Conscience is that mysterious depth within our mind that brings remorse and passionate desire for cleansing, rebirth and correction. Remorse, precisely, is the voice of conscience, and it brings us to the first step on the road to cleansing, to the desire to forgive and be forgiven, to this very "forgiveness" Sunday. Why? Why do forgiveness and the thirst for forgiveness enter us so clearly the moment our conscience is aroused, as its foremost demand? The answer is that conscience also reveals to us that the very essence of evil and falsehood is division, that it is guilt before other human beings.

Dostoevsky said through the elder Zosima that "Each is guilty of everything before everyone." At first glance these words seem not only grossly exaggerated, but simply absurd. "How am I guilty before others?," our offended reason, our "outer" mind, asks defiantly. As far as "morality" is concerned, our reason can probably agree that yes, somehow, I am in fact guilty toward someone, but, it adds comfortingly, isn't that just part of life? Let's allow reason to doubt, let's even allow morality to explain and rationalize. But let's also listen to conscience: there, deep, deep within us a quiet voice says so firmly, so insistently, "guilty." What is this guilt about? No, it's not about particular offenses and quarrels, which are, I think, quite unavoidable. It's not about trivial squabbles or petty irritations. No, this guilt which so suddenly and so obviously becomes apparent to me has its source elsewhere: in my own life, so thoroughly permeated with self love. The guilt therefore, is focused on myself; the "other" and "others" have really nothing to do with it, except insofar as they simply become means to an end. Even our love is poisoned from within, mutilated by "selfishness," as if even in love we could possess the loved one for ourselves alone.

It is the conscience, only the conscience, which suddenly reveals to us with ruthless clarity the whole world as the struggle of everyone against everyone else, a struggle which consumes life from beginning to end. Only in feeling this and becoming aware of it can we begin to hear inwardly the truth of Dostoevsky's words, "Each is guilty of everything before everyone." We can begin then to hear as well the truth of other words said before Dostoevsky, by Saint Seraphim of Sarov: "Save yourself, and thousands around you will be saved..." Save yourself: but this means precisely to save yourself first of all from this primordial slavery to division, from this inner divorce from life and from people, from this conscious or unconscious state of struggle in which we live.

To forgive and be forgiven! This is exactly how we turn from division to unity, from hostility to love, from separation to unification. But to forgive is not simply to ignore shortcomings, as we so often claim, or worse, to altogether dismiss others with the wave of a hand as hopeless and not worth the trouble. Forgiveness does not mean indifference or scorn or cynicism. Only someone who has suddenly realized with all his soul the full horror of love's absence from the world, who has felt the bottomless grief of that loneliness to which man has condemned himself by his self-affirmation and self-love—only they are capable of forgiving and being forgiven.

All of this is expressed, all of this is heard in the Church's prayer of Forgiveness Sunday: "Turn not your face away from your child, for I am afflicted..." There it is, that bright sadness, which alone enables us to finally understand the root, essence and power of evil: cold hearts, withered love, and the triumph in this world of individual self-affirmation, which can only end in isolation and loneliness. We pray for forgiveness, we thirst to be forgiven... In the same way that a little child who wrongs his mother longs for the lost paradise of her love, so each of us knows that the destruction of evil begins with this conversion of soul, with this softening of heart, with this thirst for reconciliation. And therefore, no matter how far this seems from our cold, cruel life, in which the binding force of the "collective" tightens rather than tempers each person's loneliness, no matter how foreign this seems to the very spirit of our times, it is only here, in the power of conscience, in the thirst for forgiveness and conversion of soul, that we find the beginning of our spiritual rebirth.

11

The Lenten Prayer of St Ephrem
the Syrian

Sloth, Despair, Lust of Power

For the great majority of believers, Great Lent is identified above all with the short prayer named after St Ephrem the Syrian, one of the eastern Christian teachers of the fourth century. This prayer is read at the end of every lenten service, and the faithful read it at home as part of their personal prayers. It expresses most accurately, concisely and simply the meaning and spirit of what Christians have for centuries called Great Lent.

> O Lord and Master of my life, do not give me the spirit of sloth, despair, lust of power and idle talk; but give rather the spirit of chastity, humility, patience and love to your servant. Yea, O Lord and King, grant that I may see my own transgressions and not judge my brother, for blessed are You unto ages of ages. Amen.

These are ancient words. But let us try to penetrate behind the ancient surface into their meaning and essence, just as some fifty to sixty years ago scholars first learned how to remove the surface dust and grime from ancient Russian icons. What before was dark (so dark, in fact, that the Russian writer Vasilii Rozanov even entitled his book on the Orthodox Church, *Dark Image*) was suddenly illumined and enlivened, radiating such striking colors, such joy and light, that everything we had previously understood not only about icons, but about the spiritual tone and style of Orthodoxy and ancient Russian piety, changed forever. The same can and must be done not only with icons, but with other fundamental expressions of faith and religion. Its enemies want to banish religion to museums, to convince people to equate it with the obsolete ideas and perceptions of antiquity, to prove it unnecessary.

But is this true? Let's return to the prayer of St Ephrem the Syrian. Let's listen carefully to this most simple petition of a man who recognizes the falsehood of his life and its content: "Do not give me the spirit of sloth, despair, lust of power and idle talk." First, "do not give me": protect me, defend me, deliver me. From what? From shortcomings that appear so ordinary and trivial, such as the spirit of sloth? "And anyway, what sloth can we possibly confess," says a person in contemporary society, "when every one of us is exhausted from work, when the pace of life is getting faster and faster all the time, when a little sloth, it would seem, is precisely what we need most of all?" But in this prayer the word "sloth" does not at all mean inactivity or physical rest; above all it means emptiness. "Deliver me from the spirit of emptiness." Here we are immediately shown the first terrible disease of the human spirit: emptiness. Yes, we work, we hurry, we rush around literally from morning till night, but what is the essence, what is the meaning of all this hurry and vanity? Doesn't it sometimes happen that we suddenly stop for a moment, and then in the silence around us the emptiness and meaninglessness of our life become so clear? The words of the poet are frightening in their truth and simplicity: "Life made a loud commotion and then left." This is perhaps why we deafen ourselves with work, and why the whole world around us makes so much noise and thunder, because everyone is trying to hide this abyss of emptiness from themselves and from everyone else. But to what purpose? Where does it lead? Why? "Life made a loud commotion and then left..." So here, in this prayer, entering deeply within ourselves and catching a glimpse of this so very brief gift of life, we ask to be saved and defended, to be delivered from the root of all evil: from emptiness, from meaninglessness, from the terrible bankruptcy of soul in which we so often exist...

The "...spirit of sloth, despair..." After sloth and emptiness, the inevitable result is despair. Why have all teachers of the spiritual life, all the wise men and women who have meditated on the nature of the human spirit and consciousness, always considered despair to be the most terrible sin, the most intractable evil? What is despair? Isn't every one of us familiar with that strange erosion in energy of soul, that inexplicable sadness which suddenly descends upon everything around us, so that even the most brilliant sun-filled day becomes needless, empty, useless? We say "I feel listless," and dusk settles on the soul. This is despair. It's good if we can catch ourselves and pull ourselves together. Otherwise we simply drown the despair with whatever is at hand, work, alcohol, anything... But it comes back, it is always somewhere here, waiting for the opportune moment, threatening from around the corner. It returns because in the deepest, most hidden part of our soul, in spite of attempts to hide it even

from ourselves, each of us somehow recognizes the
meaninglessness of a life which comes up against death.
"We are continually questioning, questioning," wrote the
poet Heinrich Heine, "until a lump of earth plugs-up our
throat; but could that be the answer?" When that insight
pierces to the surface through the noise and vanity of life,
then everything around us seems so meaningless, so vain,
so needless and fruitless. And from out of this experience
comes the prayer: "deliver us from despair." This isn't
helplessness or fear, as the enemies of religion suppose;
it is the one response worthy of human beings, to look this
despair right in the face, not to hide from it, but to seek
the means to overcome it...

The "spirit of sloth, despair, lust of power..." The
prayer shifts to another level of human existence, to a
different "key" to its tragedy. "Lust of power" does not
simply mean love of power and authority over other
people, since in this simple and pure form lust of power
is perhaps not seen all that often. But in another and much
deeper form, it is characteristic of each of us and is the
source of terrible injustice in human life. To have lust of
power is to relate to another human being as the means to
an end, how he or she can be used. In other terms, lust of
power is the inner subordination of everyone and everything to myself, looking at them only from the point of
view of my needs, of my interests, of me as the highest
and only value.

Idle Talk

Idle talk seems to be such a small, insignificant short-
coming. What really is so terrible about this? Banter,
wisecracking, chit-chat...We are all people, we are all

human beings, we all engage in these transgressions, but
certainly there must be sins a lot more terrible than these.
That's how it appears to us and how we've become accustomed to thinking. But the gospels say that "men will
render account for every careless word they utter" (Mt
12:36), and therefore we begin to wonder if "idle talk" is
as simple and innocent as it seems...

Each of us, if we think carefully and concretely about
our own life, and not just in terms of abstract theories,
will be convinced immediately that words, either spoken
to us or by us, have without question caused the most
suffering, the most bad blood, and poisoned more min-
utes, hours and days than anything else. Slander, incrimi-
nation, betrayal, treachery, lies, rumors—all of these are
frightening phenomena, and all of them occur exclusively
by means of words; this alone should be enough for us to
feel their terrible power. True, words can express and
create goodness, beauty, and wisdom. But they also destroy goodness, beauty and wisdom. A word can poison
the soul and fill it with suspicion, fear, malice, hatred and
cynicism. And this of course applies beyond our personal
life, for we live in an age where "idle talk" is truly of
cosmic proportions. Newspapers, radio, television,
books, schools, all of these are the instruments and almost
symbols of a grandiose, continuous, incessant "idle talk,"
whose duty is to hammer at our heads and fill them with
strange ideas, and force us to think in step with "thought
police." We can say without any exaggeration that the
world has been poisoned by "idle talk," which in the final
analysis is always a lie.

Christianity considers the gift of words to be one of
the highest, truly divine gifts bestowed upon humanity,

setting us as verbal beings apart from nonverbal beings. It calls God himself "the Word," saying in the gospel, "In the beginning was the Word and the Word was with God and the Word was God" (Jn 1:1). But it is precisely because Christianity values the word so highly and endows it with such great creative power, that it looks with such horror at the empty word, "idle talk," the word's betrayal of itself—when instead of being an instrument of goodness and light it becomes an instrument of evil and darkness... "Men will render account for every careless word they utter; for by your words you will be justified, and by your words you will be condemned" (Mt 12:36-37). Every one of us would pay dearly if only that life-poisoning word could be taken back as if never said... It is necessary to recall and feel all this in order to understand why the Prayer of St Ephrem the Syrian puts "idle talk" together with sloth, despair and lust of power as one of the four basic sins and fundamental evils. When the word is purified and restored to its first-created power, then life itself begins to be purified, restored. We speak of "weighing every word." Yes, precisely weighing, not only on the scales of caution, usefulness and calculation; but also weighing every word on the scales of justice, goodness and truth.

Chastity, Humility, Patience

In the prayer of St Ephrem the Syrian we ask God to give us a "spirit of chastity, humility, patience and love." Let's consider each of these concepts, which taken together are the foundation and source of goodness, according to Christian spiritual experience since ancient times, just as the negative petitions of the lenten prayer are the basis of sin and evil.

The spirit of chastity. The word "chastity" [*tselomudrie*], which originally was one of the deepest, most beautiful words in human language, gradually lost its "fragrance," so to say, or at any rate its meaning has shrunk. For the vast majority it now refers almost exclusively to sexual purity, as the antithesis of sexual license and debauchery. But the original meaning of the word chastity is immeasurably broader and deeper. The key to this meaning is found in two concepts which are joined together in the one Russian word *tselomudrie* (chastity): *tselostnost'* or "wholeness," and *mudrie* or "wisdom." "Chastity" is thus one of the most Christian of words, for it expresses Christianity's central experience, that goodness—the good, righteous, and authentic life—is precisely wholeness, and therefore wisdom. Wholeness stands opposed to evil, which is always a rupture, a division, a corruption of the original wholeness, and thus a departure from wisdom. The spirit of chastity is therefore that wholeness outside of which, by definition, nothing else remains. It is a return to life as wholeness. It is the joy of newly acquired wholeness, or in other terms, the peace and harmony of spirit, mind, heart and body, the joy of wisdom, the joy of "whole-wisdom."

After chastity comes "humility" [*smirennomudrie*]. And once again, notice that it is not merely humility [*smirenie*], but literally "humble wisdom" [*smirennomudrie*], for the word humility, like chastity, can be understood in a variety of ways. It can have a subservient tone to express a person's disdain for themselves as a human being, and so disdain for human beings in general: "I am so so small, so bad, so weak." No, none of this self-contempt has anything in common with true Christian humility, which is rooted in the experience of life's boundless depth. This humility comes not from ignorance and weakness, but from awe, from wisdom, from comprehension—and so it is truly from God. It is precisely fallen man who continually feels the need for pride, for self-exaltation, for self-affirmation, for a smoke screen to hide his shortcomings from others and even from himself. Those who are genuinely good, genuinely wise and genuinely alive have no need of pride, since they have nothing to hide, and therefore they are humble. Christ, the Son of God says, "Learn from me, for I am gentle and humble of heart" (Mt 11:29). And therefore in humility, as in wholeness, genuine wisdom is revealed, radiates and triumphs as "humble wisdom" [*smirennomudrie*].

Following chastity and humility comes the spirit of patience. Why does Christianity put this on such a pedestal? What is the virtue of patience? These are important questions, because Christianity and religion are accused by their opponents of preaching patience above all else. By preaching patience here, they say, and promising in return a reward there, you religious people are diverting people from fighting for freedom, you're resigning them to evil and injustice, you're turning them into obedient slaves. But they have missed the point: we are not speaking of that kind of patience. Here, in the lenten prayer, patience is an outcome of faith, trust and love; this is quite the opposite of dismissing everything with a wave of one's hand and telling oneself "I can't do anything except be patient." No, patience means first of all God himself, who did not "wave us aside," but continues to believe us, to believe in us. And this patience only comes from faith that good is stronger than evil, that love is stronger than hate, and finally, that life is stronger than death... It is for this divine virtue, this divine gift of patience, that we pray, so that we would not be shaken in our trust, nor give in to indifference, aloofness, or that dismissing wave of the hand... About both of these last qualities, humility and patience, we will have more to say in the next talk.

Humility, Patience, and Love

When you say aloud the word "humility," you feel at once how foreign it is to the spirit of modern life. What humility can we speak of when all life today is built exclusively on self-admiration and self-praise, on enthusiasm for external power, greatness, authority and so forth. This spirit of self-praise has permeated from top to bottom not only our political and government life, but our personal, professional, social, and literally every aspect of life. We teach our children to take pride, but rarely do we call them or ourselves to humility. What's more, one of the main accusations militant atheists continually level against Christianity is that it teaches people that being humble is the primary Christian virtue. Christianity therefore, according to them, teaches servility and submission, it humiliates and belittles human beings and their dignity.

What is most striking in these accusations is that no one ever explains what humility really is. What is Christianity teaching when it speaks about humility? Why, and in what sense does humility degrade human beings? Christ, for example, says about himself, "I am meek and humble of heart" (Mt 11:29), but it would never enter anyone's mind to claim that this is evidence of his indifference to evil, his blind submission to anyone and everyone, or his servile fear before the powers of this world.

Indeed, He stands before Pilate and tells him very simply,
"You would have no power over me if it had not been
given you from above" (Jn 19:11). Apparently, then, not
all humility is the same; so before denouncing it, one
needs to explain which humility is under discussion.

What is Christian humility? Above all, of course, it is
the feeling of truth—truth, in the first place, about myself.
Truth never degrades or humiliates, but raises and puri-
fies. Furthermore, humility means honesty about the truth,
refusal to exaggerate about ourselves in any way, aversion
to fogging the truth about ourselves in front of others.
Humility is finally the knowledge of one's place, one's
abilities and limitations, the courageous acceptance of
myself as I am... This is why, like chastity, humility is the
beginning of wisdom, and why we ask in prayer for the
gift of humility. Only someone who does not lie, who does
not exaggerate, who does not seek "image" over "being,"
who peacefully, soberly and courageously accepts and
does his work—only that person possesses wisdom. When
seen from this perspective, Christianity's preaching of
humility, far from demeaning human beings, elevates and,
most importantly, respects them. For only someone lack-
ing something needs self-praise, only someone ugly needs
to cover up, only someone weak needs to boast of
strength. Where there is freedom, there is no need for
propaganda; where there is genuine strength, there is no
need for threats; where there is genuine beauty, there is no
need for "impoverished excess of dress." This is why
humility is in such short supply in today's world and
today's human beings, and why it is that even unknow-
ingly, exhausted in a sea of lies and self-praise, they long
for humility more than for anything else...

After humility in the prayer of St Ephrem the Syrian comes patience, and here again we come up against one of the main accusations against religion. Yet in preaching patience, Christianity does not undermine man's ability to protest, to fight, to defend his rights, to yearn for a better, more just world. Here too, as with humility, it is best to look at the example of Christ. Yes, he teaches patience, "in patience you will save you souls" (Lk 21:19), but what Christ calls patience is just as far from the caricature of patience in atheist pamphlets, as Christian love is from that love of a distant and impersonal collective in whose name millions of people have been deprived of freedom.

Christian patience has its source not at all in indifference to evil, but, as strange as this may sound, in the active feeling of trust in human beings. No matter how far people fall, no matter how much they betray what is best in themselves, Christianity calls us to believe that man's essential being does not consist of evil and fall. It believes that human beings can always stand up once again, that they can return to their bright essence... In the end, patience is faith in the power of goodness.

Finally, we ask in the prayer of St Ephrem for the spirit of love. Love is the resolving chord of the prayer. In essence, the whole prayer leads toward this petition and fulfills itself here. For if we ask for liberation from sloth, despair, lust of power and idle talk, we are asking for the removal of barriers to love, barriers that prevent love from entering our heart. And chastity, humility, and patience are the building blocks, the roots, the first shoots of love. Therefore, when the word love finally falls upon our ears as if from heaven itself, we already know that love is not simply from God, but is God himself who enters our hearts, which are now cleansed and adorned with chastity, humility and patience, are now prepared to be a temple through the presence, light and all-conquering power of God's love. Love is at once both the hidden motivation of our life and its goal. Through love all is alive, toward love all is directed, and through love we come to know that God is Love.

12

The Sunday of the Cross

From time immemorial, on Saturday evening of the third week in Great Lent, a cross is brought into the center of the church, and the entire following week is known as the Week of the Cross. We know that Great Lent is the preparation for Holy Week, when the Church will recall the suffering, crucifixion and death of Jesus Christ on the cross. Bringing out the cross in the middle of Lent is therefore a reminder of the goal of our deeper and more intense religious life during Lent. So it is appropriate to reflect here on the role of the cross, this most important and most prominent of all Christian symbols.

This symbol has two closely intertwined meanings. On the one hand, it is Christ's cross, that decisive event through which the earthly life and ministry of Jesus Christ was completed. It is a story of puzzling and terrifying hatred toward the One whose entire teaching focused on the commandment of love, whose entire preaching was the call to self-denial and sacrifice in the name of this love. Pilate, the Roman governor to whom the arrested, beaten, spit-upon Christ was brought, says, "I find no crime in him" (Jn 19:4). But this provokes an even louder outburst: "Crucify him! Crucify him!" shouts the crowd. And so the cross of Christ poses an eternal question aimed at the very depth of our conscience: why does goodness arouse not only opposition, but hatred? Why is goodness always crucified in this world? We usually avoid answering this question by placing the blame on someone else: if we had been there, if I had been there that terrible night, I would not have behaved as everybody else. But, alas, somewhere deep in our conscience we know that is not true. We know that the people who tortured, crucified and hated Christ were not monsters of some sort, possessed by some peculiar and unique evil. No, they were essentially "just like everybody else." Pilate even tried to defend Jesus, to dissuade the crowd; he even offered to release Christ as a goodwill gesture in honor of the holiday; when that failed he stood in front the crowd and washed his hands, showing his disagreement with this murder.

In a few strokes, the gospel draws for us a picture of this pathetic Pilate, his fright, his bureaucratic conscience, his cowardly refusal to follow his own conscience. Isn't this also exactly what happens in our own life and in life around us? Isn't this the most commonplace, the most typical of all stories? Isn't Pilate present within us all the time? Isn't it true that when the moment comes for us to say a decisive, irrevocable no to falsehood, injustice, evil and hate, we give in to the temptation to "wash our hands"? Behind Pilate were the Roman soldiers, but they could certainly say in their own defense: we only followed orders, we were told to "neutralize" some trouble-maker who was causing disruption and disorder, so what's there to talk about? Behind Pilate, behind the soldiers, was the crowd, the same people who

six days before had cried out "Hosanna" as they trium-
phantly welcomed Christ as He entered Jerusalem—only
now their cry is "Crucify Him!" But they too have an
explanation. Didn't the leaders, the teachers, the authorities tell them that this man was a criminal who broke the
laws and customs, and therefore by law (always by law,
always according to the appropriate statute) must die...
And so each of the participants in this terrible event was
right "in their own eyes," since each had justification. Yet
together, they all murdered a man in whom there was
"found no crime." The first meaning of the cross, therefore, is its judgment of evil, or rather, of this world's
pseudo-goodness, in which evil eternally rejoices, and
which promotes evil's terrifying triumph on earth.

This brings us to the second meaning of the cross.
After Christ's cross comes my cross, of which Christ
said, "If any man would come after me, let him...take up
his cross daily and follow me" (Lk 9:23). This means that
the choice everyone faced that night—Pilate, the soldiers,
the leaders, the crowd and every person in that crowd—is
a choice that is continually, daily set before each of us.
Outwardly, the choice may come through something apparently insignificant to us, something secondary. But to
conscience there is neither primary nor secondary, only
truth and falsehood, good and evil. To take up one's cross
daily is not merely to endure life's burdens and cares, but
above all to live in harmony with conscience, to live
within the light of the judgment of conscience.

Even today, with the whole world looking on, a person "who has no crime in him" can be taken away, tortured, beaten, put in prison or sent into exile. And all of
this according to law, all according to obedience and

discipline, all in the name of good order, for the good of all. And how many Pilates are washing their hands, how many soldiers are hurrying to carry out the orders of military discipline, how many people obediently, submissively cheer them on, or at best watch silently as evil triumphs?

As we bring out the cross, as we bow down before it, as we kiss it, let's recall its meaning. What does it tell us, to what does it call us? Let's remember the cross as a choice on which everything else in the world hangs, and without which everything the world is a triumph of darkness and evil. "For judgment I came into this world," Christ said (Jn 9:39). At this judgment, before the tribunal of crucified love, truth and goodness, each of us stands trial.

13

Death

As Easter approaches, thoughts almost involuntarily focus on a subject which is so stubbornly minimized by secular media and antireligious propaganda, but which in one way or another unavoidably stands at the center of human consciousness, the subject of death. For Christians, Easter is the feast of victory over death, "Trampling down death by death." In past ages of Christianity's outward triumph, when Easter was the self-evident focus of the year, when its joy and gladness were shared by people as their own foremost joy, this celebration and its meaning needed no explanation. But today, for someone who knows little or nothing of what occurs on Easter night, who has not experienced that peculiar and joyful thrill when out of the darkness comes the first proclamation of "Christ is risen," Easter has of course ceased being what it was for centuries: the proof, witness, and symbol of genuine victory over the darkness, sadness and hopelessness of death.

Antireligious propaganda likes to claim that one of the sources for religion is fear of death: people were afraid of death and so they invented immortality of the soul, the world to come, eternity and so forth. The reality, of course, is that none of this exists. With physical death,

human beings utterly disappear and turn into nothingness. It has always surprised me how fiercely and with
what inexpréssible inspiration the propaganda fights for
this nothingness. They make it seem that dissolving into
nothingness is very good, just fantastic; while on the
other hand, faith in eternity and immortality are somehow
dangerous and must be combatted with all possible force.
Yet it appears to me that even if one could prove death to
be the absolute end, after which there is nothing else, that
this finally brings little joy. So someone lives, studies,
suffers, feels inspired, loves, and then it's all gone, as if
he were never here. And therefore, it would seem that
man's eternal, indestructible dream of immortality, this
desire for immortality, is something good, noble, and
worthy of respect. But no! Nothing, it seems, is so hated
by anti-religious propaganda as the idea of immortality
and faith in man's eternity.

But let's consider the subject rationally. First of all,
religion should not be ashamed of being concerned with
death, or even of being accused that fear of death gave
birth to religion. Death is too important a human phenomenon to be ignored or dismissed, as in antireligious
propaganda, as if there really is nothing to think about
here, and the latest five-year plan is much more important. Fear of death is part of being human, because people
instinctively feel a kind of terrifying, one could say awe-
inspiring, discord between the experience of one's own
self and the knowledge that this self must die and come to
an end. No matter how often I'm told that death is a
natural event, an obvious law of nature, my own self feels
that its own death is not only unnatural, but contrary to
nature. This discord gives birth to fear, because every-

thing strange or unnatural is frightening. And in spite of all we are told of the naturalness of death, the fear connected with it is the best proof that everything here is not so clear and simple. It is natural for human beings to desire what is natural. But death, disappearance, dissolving into nothingness, "a black pit with spiders," as Dostoevsky said, the deafening sink-hole of non-existence is something no one desires.

Everywhere, death always remains a mystery which human beings, insofar as they are human and not machines, robots, or ants, cannot but look and reflect upon. Attempts, therefore, to simply remove this subject and replace it with discussion about economics or politics not only fail, but testify to shallowness and narrow-mindedness. And when we're told to overcome fear of death by working for future generations and their happiness, none of the propaganda recognizes how incredibly stupid this is. For if we accept that human tragedy is grounded in the awareness of our own death, then this tragedy continues also in the future, regardless of the material happiness of those famous future generations. If human beings are doomed to nothingness, if the end of each person (and certainly there is no humanity in general, only people) is nothingness, then permit me to ask: how does this awful absurdity become any less absurd in the future with, let's suppose, more justice and better home heating? But no philosophy, no ideology based on rejection of immortality and eternity can promise anything more. If nothingness is human destiny, then the proponents of so-called "existentialism" are much more logical and honest; they simply begin with the premise that human life is absurd and meaningless. And then, of course, what Leo Tolstoy said, "after a stupid life comes a stupid death," has more truth than the endless plans and discussions by cheap ideologies of future happiness.

All this brings us to a simple affirmation: death is an extremely important subject for human beings to ponder and attempt to understand. In some profound sense, the whole of a person's life revolves around solving the riddle of his mysterious end. Religion's depth lies in its refusal to avoid this subject. But antireligious propaganda hides from people the actual religious teaching about death, and particularly Christian teaching. It equates this teaching with pre-historic and primitive "animism," and most importantly, it conceals the fact that Christianity's true inspiration lies not in reconciliation with death, but in fighting and overcoming it.

14

Palm Sunday

Great Lent is completed and comes to an end with two bright, festal days, or rather, a two-in-one, two-day feast. This is Lazarus Saturday, recalling Christ's raising of his dead friend Lazarus, and Palm Sunday, when we celebrate Christ's triumphal entrance into Jerusalem six days before he was betrayed to suffer and die on the cross. In these two bright days, the Church reveals to us the authentic meaning of Christ's voluntary sacrifice and saving death before we enter the sadness and darkness of the passion, before we once again become witnesses of Christ's suffering.

Christ was far from Jerusalem when Lazarus died, and it was not until four days later that he arrived in Bethany and met Lazarus' sisters, Martha and Mary, and his weeping and grieving friends. The gospel of St John recounts this meeting in detail, beginning with his conversation with Martha and Mary. Both of them tell Christ, "Lord, if you had been here, my brother would not have died..." (Jn 11:21, 32). And Christ answers: "Your brother will rise again" (Jn 11:23). But regardless of this answer, when He saw the weeping of the sisters and their friends, He himself "was deeply moved in spirit and troubled..." (Jn 11:33). Approaching the grave, He himself wept, and those around said, "see how he loved him!" (Jn 11:36). Christ ordered that the stone lying against the grave be taken away. And when they had removed the stone, "He cried with a loud voice, 'Lazarus, come forth!' The dead man came out, his hands and feet bound with bandages..." (Jn 11:43-44). What is the meaning of this event which the Church celebrates so brightly, so joyfully, so victoriously on Lazarus Saturday? How can we reconcile Christ's sadness and tears with his power to raise the dead? Through its entire celebration, the Church replies that Christ weeps because, in seeing the death of his friend, He sees also death's victory over the whole world; He sees that death, which God did not create, has usurped the throne and now rules over the world, poisoning life, turning everything into a meaningless stream of days flowing mercilessly towards the abyss. Then comes this command, "Lazarus, come forth!" Here is the miracle of love triumphant over death, a summons announcing Christ's declaration of war on death, a vow that death itself will be destroyed and put to death. And in order to destroy death and its darkness, Christ himself, and this means God himself, love itself, life itself, descends into the grave to encounter death face to face in order to annihilate it and to give us the eternal life God created us to possess.

The next day Christ enters Jerusalem. But this time He doesn't enter as He did before, unrecognized, unknown, unacknowledged. No, now He himself, who never before sought either power or glory, prepares for his triumph. He orders his disciples to bring a young donkey, and sitting upon it He enters the city preceded by a crowd and children bearing palm branches in their hands. The crowd and the children greet him with an ancient greeting reserved only for the king: "'Hosanna...! Blessed is He that comes in the name of the Lord! Hosanna in the highest!' And when he entered Jerusalem all the city was stirred..." (Mt 21:9-10). This crowd, these palm branches, that thunderous royal welcome, that triumphant joy, what does it all mean? And why do we commemorate this event each year with exactly the same joy, as if we ourselves were standing on the street of that holy city waiting, welcoming, exulting, and repeating the very same words, the very same "Hosanna"? This means that Christ was a king, if only of a single city far away from us. It means that He reigned, that the people recognized Him as a king! Yes, He taught about the Kingdom of God and about his future reign. But on this day, six days before Passover, He reveals his kingdom on earth, He opens it, inviting the people, and all of us as well, to become citizens of this Kingdom of Christ, subjects of this humble King, a King with no earthly authority, with no earthly might, but with all-powerful love.

We live in a world, under governments, that have renounced God and are busy only with themselves, jealously guarding their own authority, power, might and victories. There is almost no place in this world for God's love, God's light, God's joy. But on this one day of the year, when we stand in overflowing churches, raising up our palm branches and hearing once again the thunder of that royal Hosanna, we say to ourselves and to the world: Christ's Kingdom lives. The kingdom that shone so brightly on that day in Jerusalem has not died, it has not perished, it has not disappeared from the face of the earth. We say to God: You are the one Lord, You are our only

King; we know and believe and affirm that this Kingdom of your love will be victorious over sin, evil, and death. The joy of this faith no one can take from us, even if others put all their hope in power and violence, even if their only belief is in bullets, prisons, terror, and torture. No, this kingdom of violence, evil and lies will not stand. It will collapse, as every previous kingdom has collapsed, as every previous tyrant has vanished. But your Kingdom, Lord, will remain. And the time will come when with your love You will wipe every tear from our eyes, dissolve every sorrow in your joy, and fill the world You created with the light of immortality.

After his victory on Palm Sunday, we know that Christ begins his descent to suffering and death. But the torch lit on this day will illumine even that abysmal darkness. Beyond the cross and death arises the dawn of inexpressible resurrection joy. This, then, is the meaning and power of those remarkable two days when, after completing Lent, we prepare to follow Christ to his voluntary passion, to his victorious descent into death, and to his all-glorious resurrection on the third day.

15

Christic Risen!

On Easter night, when the paschal procession outside the church stops in front of the closed doors, during that last moment of silence before the eruption of resurrection joy, a question rises in our hearts consciously or unconsciously. It is the very same question that was in the hearts of the women who, early in the morning "just as the sun had risen," first came to Christ's tomb: "Who will roll away the stone for us from the door of the tomb?" Will this miracle take place once again? Will the night once again become brighter than the day? Will we once again be filled with that inexplicable joy which is so utterly independent of anything in this world, that joy which all this night and for many days to come will ring out in the embrace of the paschal greeting: "Christ is risen! Truly He is risen!" That moment always comes. The doors open. We step into a church now filled with light, and we enter the triumphant service of Easter Matins.

But somewhere within the soul a question remains. What does all this mean? What does it mean to celebrate Easter in this world filled with suffering, hatred, triviality and war? What does it mean to sing of "trampling down death by death" and to hear that "not one dead remains in the grave," when death, disregarding all our day-to-day hurry, still remains the one absolute earthly certainty... Is it possible that Easter, this radiant and triumphant night, is merely a momentary escape from reality, a spiritual drinking binge after which, sooner or later, the same routine will return, the same gray reality, the same pitiless checking-off of days, months, years, the same race toward death and non-existence? After all, we've been told for such a long time that religion is self-deception and opium, an invention to help man cope with his hard fate, an ever-dissolving mirage. Would it not be more courageous, more worthy of man's dignity to renounce this mirage and face squarely the simple and sober reality? What is the answer to all this?

I think that the first tentative answer could be this: it's just not possible that all of this is a fabrication! It's just not possible that so much faith, so much joy, so much light over these almost two-thousand years could only be escape and mirage. Can a mirage continue for centuries? This argument has some weight, but it is still not completely convincing, and it must be stated plainly that no absolutely convincing answer exists, one that would be totally acceptable and publishable as a scientific explanation of Easter faith. Here, each person can only testify of his own personal and living experience and speak for himself. In living and personal experience, in considering it and reflecting upon it, you suddenly find the foundation of everything else, you discover what illumined everything with such blinding light and truly melts doubts and questions as wax melts before fire.

But what experience? I cannot describe or define it other than as the experience of the living Christ. My belief in Christ does not come from the opportunity given to me to participate since earliest childhood in the paschal celebration. Rather, Pascha is made possible, that unique night fills with light and joy and such victorious power in the greeting "Christ is risen! Truly He is risen!" because my faith itself was born from experience of the living Christ. How and when was it born? I don't know, I don't remember. I only know that every time I open the gospel and read about Christ, read his words, read his teaching, I consciously repeat, with all my heart and being, what was said by those who were sent to arrest Christ but who returned to the Pharisees without him: "No man ever spoke like this man" (Jn 7:46). Therefore what I know first of all is that Christ's teaching is alive, and that nothing on earth can be compared with it. And this teaching is about him, about eternal life, about victory over death, about a love that conquers and overcomes death. I know as well that in a life where everything seems so difficult and tiresome, the one constant that never changes and never leaves is this inner awareness that Christ is with me. "I will not leave you as orphans, I will come to you" (Jn 14:18). And he does come and give the feeling of his presence through prayer, through a thrill of soul, through a joy so incomprehensible yet so very alive, through his mysterious, but again so certain, presence in church during services and in sacraments. This living experience is always growing, this knowledge, this awareness which becomes so obvious that Christ is here and that his word has been fulfilled: whoever loves Me, "I will love him and manifest myself to him" (Jn 14:21). And whether I am in a crowd or alone, this certitude of his presence, this power of his word, this joy of faith in him remains with me. This is the only answer and the only proof.

"Why do you seek the living among the dead? Why do you mourn the incorrupt amid corruption?" All Christianity, therefore, is the experience of faith repeated again and again as if for the first time, through its incarnation in rites, words, music, and colors. To the unbeliever, it may indeed seem like a mirage; he hears only words, he sees only incomprehensible ceremonies, and he understands them only outwardly. But for believers, all of this radiates from within, and not as proof of his faith, but as its result, as its life in the world, in the soul, in history. Therefore the darkness and sadness of Holy Friday is for us something real, alive, contemporary; we can cry at the cross and experience everything that took place in that triumph of evil, treachery, cowardice, and betrayal; we can contemplate the lifebearing tomb on Holy Saturday with excitement and hope. And therefore, every year we can celebrate Easter, Pascha, the Resurrection. For Easter is not the remembrance of an event in the past. It is the real encounter in happiness and joy, with him whom our hearts long ago knew and encountered as the life and light of all light. Easter night testifies that Christ is alive and with us, and that we are alive with him. The entire celebration is an invitation to look at the world and life, and to behold the dawning of the mystical day of the Kingdom of light. "Today the scent of Spring begins," sings the church, "and the new creation exults..." It exults in faith, in love and in hope.

> This is the day of resurrection,
> Let us be illumined by the feast,
> Let us embrace each other,

Let us call "brothers" even those that hate us,
And forgive all by the resurrection,
And so let us cry: Christ is risen from the dead,
Trampling down death by death,
And upon those in the tombs bestowing life.

Christ is risen!

16

Easter Faith

In the days that follow Easter, I repeatedly and involuntarily return to the same question: if the unprecedented affirmation "Christ is risen" contains the entire essence, depth, and meaning of Christian faith; if in St Paul's words "your faith is in vain" if Christ has not been raised (1 Cor 15:14), then how does it make a difference here and now in our life, in my life? Another Pascha has come and gone. Once again we experienced that amazing night, the sea of burning candles, the growing excitement; there we were, once again, in the midst of a service of radiant joy, whose entire content was like one exultant hymn: "Now all is filled with light, heaven and earth and the lower regions. Let all creation celebrate the rising of Christ. In him we are established." What joyful, victorious words! Everything is united: heaven, earth, the underground kingdom of death. The whole world participates in this victory, and in Christ's resurrection discovers its own meaning and affirmation.

But it passes, the night is over, the celebration ends, we leave the light and return to the world, we descend back to earth and reenter the normal, everyday, sober reality of our life. And what do we find? Everything is the same, nothing has changed, and it seems that nothing, absolutely nothing has any connection whatsoever to the song we heard in church, "Let all creation celebrate the rising of Christ. In him we are established." And now doubt begins to creep into our soul. These words, so beautiful, so sublime—more beautiful and sublime than any other words on earth—could they be just an illusion, a dream? Soul and heart drink passionately of these words, but cold reason says: dreams, self-deception! Two-thousand years have gone by, and what have these words been able to do? Where is their power? Where is their victory? My goodness, how often Christians see this and just hang their heads and don't even try to fit all the pieces together. Leave us alone, they seem to tell the world, let us have our last precious possessions, comfort and joy! Don't interfere as we proclaim in church, behind closed doors, that the whole world exults. If you won't interfere with us, we won't interfere with you as you construct, direct, and live in this world any way you please...

Yet, in the deepest corner of our conscience, we know that this timidity and minimalism, this inner escape into a mystical and secret celebration is incompatible with the authentic meaning and joy of Easter. Either Christ is risen or He is not risen. One or the other! If He is risen (and why else have a paschal exultation that fills the entire night with light, triumph and victory?), if at a decisive and unique moment in human and world history, this unheard of victory over death actually occurred, then everything in the world truly has become different and new, whether people know it or not. But then we, as believers, as the ones who rejoice and celebrate, are responsible that others should know and believe, that they should see, hear and enter into this victory and this joy. The early Christians called their faith not a religion, but the Good News, which it was their purpose in the world to spread and proclaim. They knew and believed that Christ's resurrection was not merely the occasion for an annual feast, but the source of powerful and transfigured life. What they heard whispered, they shouted from the housetops (Mt 10:27)... "Yes, but what can I do," my sober and realistic reason responds. "How can I proclaim or shout or witness? I, who am just a powerless little grain of sand, lost among the masses?" But this objection by reason and "sound mind" is a lie, perhaps the most terrible and demonic lie of today's world. This world has somehow convinced us that strength and significance come only through large numbers, multitudes, the masses. What can one person do against everyone else? Yet it is right here, in opposition to this lie, that Christianity's fundamental affirmation must be brought into the open with all its force and incomparable logic. Christianity affirms that one person can be stronger than everyone else, and this affirmation is precisely the good news of Christ. Consider these remarkable verses from Boris Pasternak's "Garden of Gethsemane":

> He renounced with no hostility,
> As if returning property on loan,
> His works of wonder and his might.
> And now, like us, was mortal.

This is truly the image of Christ: a man with no authority, no hostility, no earthly power whatsoever. One man! Forsaken, betrayed, cast aside by all. But victorious. Pasternak continues:

You see, the march of centuries, like the walk to Emmaus,
Can set hearts alight along the road.
Because of its terrifying majesty
In voluntary suffering I descend into the grave.
I descend into the grave
And on the third day will arise,
And as rafts upon the river float,
So to me for judgment,
As barges in a convoy,
The centuries, out of the darkness, will come drifting by...

"Can set hearts alight along the road..." In this "set hearts alight" we find the key to answering the doubts of sober reason. What would happen if each of us who has experienced resurrection joy, who has heard its victory, who has come to believe what it has accomplished, unknown to the world, but in and for the world; if each of us, forgetting about large numbers, multitudes and masses, were to transmit this joy and this faith to just one other person, were to touch just one other human soul? If this faith and joy were secretly present in every conversation, even the most unimportant, in the sober realities of our daily life, they would immediately begin, here and now, today, to transfigure the world and life. Christ said, "The Kingdom of God is not coming with signs to be observed" (Lk 17:20). The Kingdom of God comes with power, with light, with victory, each time I and every believer carry it with us from the church into the world, and begin to live by it in our own life. Then everything, at all times, at every minute "can set hearts alight along the road..."

17

Doubting Thomas

"Unless I see...I will not believe" (Jn 20:25). So said Thomas, one of Christ's twelve disciples, in response to the joyful news of those who had seen their crucified and buried Teacher risen from the dead. Eight days later, as recorded in the gospels, when the disciples once again were all together, Christ appeared and told Thomas: "Put your finger here and see my hands; and put out your hand and place it in my side; be not faithless, but believing." And Thomas exclaimed: "My Lord and my God!" Then Christ told him: "You have believed because you have seen me; blessed are those who have not seen and yet believe..." (Jn 20:24-31).

Millions of people today think and speak essentially like Thomas, and assume that this is the only correct approach worthy of any thinking person. "Unless I see, I will not believe..." In our contemporary speech isn't this the "scientific approach"? But Christ says: "Blessed are those who have not seen and yet believe." This means that there is, and was, another approach, another standard, another possibility. True, others may say, but that approach is naive and not rational; it's unscientific; it's for people who are backward; and since I'm a person of the modern world, "Unless I see, I will not believe."

We live in a world of great oversimplification and therefore spiritual poverty. "Scientific" or "Unscientific." People use words like these all the time as if they were self-evident and self-explanatory, and they use them because everyone else also uses them, without reflection, without debate. In fact, they themselves believe these reductions blindly and simplistically, and so any other approach appears to them as neither serious nor worthy of attention. The question is already decided. But is that really true? I just said that we live in a world of great spiritual poverty. And indeed, if the end result of humanity's interminable development boils down to this pronouncement, "I won't believe it till I see it"; if the human race looks upon this as the height of wisdom and reason's greatest victory, then our world truly is poor, superficial, and most all, incredibly boring. If I only know what I see, touch, measure and analyze, then how little I really know! The whole world of the human spirit falls by the wayside, all the intuition and profound knowledge that flows not from "I see" or "I touch," but from "I think" and, most importantly, "I contemplate."

What falls away is that realm of knowledge which for centuries was rooted not in external, observable experience, but in another human faculty, an amazing and perhaps inexplicable ability that sets human beings apart from everything else and makes them truly unique. Even robots, machines and computers can now touch, handle and manipulate objects; they can make accurate observations, and even make predictions. We know that they actually perform better than human beings in measuring, comparing, making exact observations flawlessly; they are more accurate, more "scientific." But here is what no robot, under any circumstances, will ever be able to do: to be filled with wonder, to be awed, to have feelings, to be moved by tenderness, to rejoice, to see what can't be seen by measurement or analysis of any kind. No robot will hear those unheard sounds that give birth to music and poetry; no robot will ever cry, or trust. But without all this doesn't our world become colorless, boring and, I would say, unnecessary? Oh yes, planes and spaceships will fly ever further and faster. But where to and what for? Oh yes, laboratories will conduct their analyses with ever increasing accuracy. But to what end? "For the good of humanity," I'm told. I understand, so this means that one day we will have a healthy, well fed, self-satisfied human being walking about, who will be totally blind, totally deaf and totally unaware of his deafness and blindness.

"Unless I see I will not believe." Clearly, however, observable experience, empirical data, is just one form of knowledge, the most elementary, and therefore the lowest, form. Empirical analysis is useful and necessary, but to reduce all human knowledge to this level is like trying to comprehend the beauty of a painting by a chemical analysis of its paint. What we call faith is at a second and higher level of human knowledge, without which, it can be claimed, man would be unable to live even a single day. Every person believes in something or someone, so the only question is whose faith, whose vision, whose knowledge of the world corresponds more accurately and more completely to the richness and complexity of life.

Some say that the resurrection of Christ must be a fabrication since the dead do not rise. True, if there is no God. But if God exists, then death must be overthrown, since God cannot be a God of decay and death. Others will then say: but there is no God, since no one has seen him. But how then do you account for the experience of millions of people who joyfully affirm that they have seen, not with their physical eyes, but with a profound and certain inner sight? Two thousand years have passed, but when the joyful proclamation "Christ is risen!" descends as if from heaven, all still send out the same triumphant response, "Truly He is risen!"

Is it really true that you neither see nor hear? Is it really true that in the deepest part of your consciousness, away from all analysis, measurements and palpation, you neither see nor feel an undying, radiant light, you do not hear the sounds of an eternal voice: "I am the way, the resurrection and the life..."? Is it really true that in the depth of your soul you do not recognize Christ within us, within me, answering Doubting Thomas, "Blessed are those who have not seen, and yet believe"?

18

The Myrrhbearing Women

Listening to the account of Christ's crucifixion and death during Holy Week, I am invariably struck by one detail in the story: the loyalty to the very end of a handful of people, mostly women, about whom the gospels tell us almost nothing else. What we do know is that Christ's disciples, all of them, ran away and left him behind. Peter denied him three times. Judas betrayed him. Crowds followed Christ while he was preaching, and each person was expecting to get something from him: they expected help, miracles and healings; they expected liberation from hated Roman occupation; they expected him to put their earthly cares in order. These countless people poorly understood the meaning of His teaching, if they even really heard it at all, of self-renunciation and love, of wholehearted self-giving. For them, Christ was a handout, an offer of help, and so they came and followed. But then came growing hatred toward him on the part of the national leaders and those in authority. In Christ's preaching of love the crowds now began to hear him foretelling that, through this love, He would offer himself as a sacrifice. And the crowd began to thin, to melt away. Christ's earthly glory and human success burst into bright flame for the last time on the day of his triumphant entry into Jerusalem, when, in the words of the gospel, "all the city was stirred" (Mt 21:10). But that was only for a moment. And even then, didn't the crowds greet him with such joy and enthusiasm only because, once again, they wanted and expected him to give them an earthly kingdom, earthly victory, power, and glory?

All of this suddenly ended. The light went out, and after Palm Sunday came the darkness, loneliness and inconsolable grief of Holy Week. And was not the most painful part of these final days the betrayal by close friends and disciples to whom Christ had truly given himself totally? In the garden of Gethsemane, even the three disciples closest to him did not stand firm, but fell asleep while Christ was in final agony, sweating blood and preparing for a horrible death. We know that even Peter, who so loudly promised to die with Christ, wavered at the last moment and renounced, rejected and betrayed him. And "Then," writes the evangelist, "all the disciples forsook him and fled" (Mt 26:56).

But not all, as it turned out. The Cross brings on the hour of simple human faithfulness and love. Those who in time of "success" seemed so removed, whom we almost never meet in the pages of the gospels, to whom Christ had given no advance word of his resurrection, and for whom therefore everything ended and was lost on the night of the Cross—these were the people who proved faithful, who remained at the Cross in steadfast human love. The evangelist John writes, "Standing by the Cross of Christ were His mother, and His Mother's sister, Mary the wife of Clopas, and Mary Magdalene" (Jn 19:25). Later, after the death of Jesus,

When it was evening, there came a rich man from Arimathea, named Joseph, who also was a disciple of Jesus. He went to Pilate and asked for the body of Jesus. Then Pilate ordered it to be given to him. And Joseph took the body, and wrapped it in a clean linen shroud, and laid it in his own new tomb, which he had hewn in the rock; and he rolled a great stone to the door of the tomb, and departed. (Mt 27:57-60)

One day later, after the sabbath, at dawn on the third day, the same women came to the grave, in keeping with the custom of that time, to anoint the dead body with aromatic spices. And it was precisely to them that the risen Christ first appeared. They were the first to hear from him that "Rejoice" which forever afterwards became the essence of Christian strength. Christ had not revealed the mystery of the future to these women, as He did to the twelve chosen apostles. They knew neither the meaning of his death nor the mystery of his approaching victory in the resurrection. For them, the death of their teacher and friend was simply death, the end; even worse, it was a terrible and shameful death, a terrible and abrupt end. They stood at the Cross only because they loved Jesus, and in loving him, suffered with him. They did not leave his poor, tortured body, but did all that love has always done at final separation.

Those whom Christ had asked to stay with him at the hour of his agonizing struggle, when He "began to be greatly distressed and troubled" (Mk 14:33), dropped him, ran away and renounced him. But those from whom He asked nothing remained faithful in their simple human love. "Mary stood weeping outside the tomb" (Jn 20:11). Down through the centuries, love has always wept in this way, as Christ wept at the grave of his friend Lazarus.

Here then, it is this love which first learns of the victory; this love, this faithfulness is the first to know that there is no longer any need for weeping, for "death is swallowed up in victory" (1 Cor 15:54), and hopeless separation is no more.

This is what the Sunday of the Myrrhbearing Women means. It reminds us that the love and faithfulness of a few individuals shone brightly in the midst of hopeless darkness. It calls us to ensure that in this world love and faithfulness do not disappear or die out. It judges our lack of courage, our fear, our endless and servile rationalizations. The mysterious Joseph and Nicodemus, and these women who go to the grave at dawn, occupy so little space in the gospels. Precisely here, however, is where the eternal fate of each of us is decided.

Today, I think, we are especially in need of recovering this love and basic human loyalty. For we have entered a time when even these are being discredited by harmful concepts of the person and human life now prevailing in this world. For centuries, the world still had the weak, but still flickering and shining, glow from that faithfulness, love and co-suffering which was silently present at the sufferings of the Man cast aside by all. And we need to cling, as if to a last thread, to everything in our world that still thrives on the warm light of simple, earthly, human love. Love does not ask about theories and ideologies, but speaks to the heart and soul. Human history has rumbled along, kingdoms have risen and fallen, cultures have been built and bloody wars fought, but what has remained unchanging on earth and in this troubled and tragic history is the bright image of the woman. An image of care, self-giving, love, compassion. Without this presence, without this light, our world, regardless of its successes and accomplishments, would be a world of terror. It can be said without exaggeration that the humanity of the human race was, and is, being preserved, saved, by woman—preserved not by words or ideas, but by her silent, caring, loving presence. And if, despite all the evil that dominates the world, the mysterious feast of life still continues, if it is still celebrated in a poverty-stricken room, at a barren table, just as joyously as in a palace, then the joy and light of this feast is in her, in woman, in her never-fading love and faithfulness. "The wine gave out..." (Jn 2:3), but while she is here—mother, wife, bride—there is enough wine, enough love, enough light for everyone...

19

The Sunday of the Paralytic

On the third Sunday after Easter, the reading from the gospel of John recounts Christ's healing of a paralytic. "There was a feast," writes the Evangelist John, and Jesus went up to Jerusalem. Now there is in Jerusalem by the Sheep Gate a pool, in Hebrew called Bethsaida, which has five porticoes. In these lay a multitude of invalids, blind, lame, paralyzed waiting for the moving of the water; for an angel of the Lord went down at certain seasons into the pool, and troubled the water: whoever stepped in first after the troubling of the water was healed of whatever disease he had. One man was there, who had been ill for thirty-eight years. When Jesus saw him and knew that he had been lying there a long time, he said to him, "Do you want to be healed?" The sick man answered him, "Sir, I have no man to put me into the pool when the water is troubled, and while I am going another steps down before me." Jesus said to him, "Rise, take up your pallet, and walk." And at once the man was healed, and he took up his pallet and walked. (Jn 5:1-9)

That is the gospel record, and having heard it, many will respond that it's just another miracle, another unbelievable event that has nothing whatsoever in common with our life, interests, needs, questions... But we listen carefully and reflect: the gospel is so childishly simple, and its stories so short, that a person of today is easily fooled by this brevity and simplicity. It seems to him or her that the truth about themselves and about their life must be complicated and cumbersome, because they themselves are complicated. But perhaps the gospel's ageless power resides in its reduction of everything to the most essential, elementary, fundamental: good and evil, darkness and light, man and God, life and death. And indeed, any focused and deep thought that involves not merely the mind, but one's entire being, in the end always concerns what is most essential. For all of life's complexity balances on the simplicity of eternal questions: good and evil, life and death, God and man.

So, in this particular gospel story, what is eternal and enduring? At its center, very clearly, are the paralytic's words to Christ, "I have no man." This truly is the cry of someone who has come to know the terrible power of human selfishness, narcissism. Every man for himself. Looking out for number one. All of them, all that great multitude of blind, sick, paralyzed, are all "waiting for the troubling of the waters," in other words, waiting for help, concern, healing, comfort. But...each waits by himself, for himself. And when the waters are troubled, each throws himself forward and forgets about the others... From the gospel's point of view, this pool is of course an image of the world, an image of human society, a symbol of the very organization of human consciousness.

Oh, of course, within the world one can find many examples of people who overcome egoism, examples of goodness and self-sacrifice. But even when someone has apparently overcome personal selfishness, he is still held prisoner by the category "his." He may have overcome bondage to himself as an individual, but then it is "his" family, and for "his" family, since "charity begins at home." If not family, then "his" ethnic group or country. If not this, then "his" social class, "his" political party. His, always his! And this "his" is invariably opposed to someone else's, which by definition becomes alien and hostile. We're told that this is how the world works, what can you do? But is this really true, is this really the ultimate, objective, and scientific truth about the person and human life?

Is it really true that everything in this world boils down to personal or collective self-interest, and that everyone lives by this? We are told that capitalism is wrong because it is self-serving and must, therefore, be destroyed in the name of communism. But self-serving is exactly what communism has been, constantly trumpeting its own worldview, its own class, its own party and so forth: its own against not-its-own, the other... And there is no escape whatsoever from this vicious cycle.

Unknown to us, however, we no longer feel suffocated by this world so totally drunk on all-consuming ego. We have become accustomed to blood, hatred, violence and, at best, indifference. Sometime in the 1920's, a young man, practically a boy, left a note and then committed suicide: "I do not want to live in a world where everyone is playing a con game..." All of this was suffocating him, he could not stand it any longer. But we are gradually harassed into accepting this as normal, and the horror of self-centeredness we cease experiencing as horrible... This is what the gospel story of the paralytic is about. All these sick, helpless, paralyzed people are sick first and foremost with incurable narcissism. This is what brings a person to cry: "I have no man!" There is no one! And this means that a person comes into being when narcissism is overcome; it means that human beings, above all, are a face turned toward the other person, eyes looking intently with concern and love into the eyes of the other person. It is love, co-suffering and care. The gospel also tells us that this new and authentic human being has been revealed to us, has come to us in Christ. In him, the One who comes to the lonely and long-suffering paralytic is no stranger, but "his own"; He comes in order to take up the sick man's sufferings as his own, his life as his own, to help and to heal.

"Do you want to be healed?" This is not the question of someone intent on forcing, convincing or subduing others. It is the question of genuine love, and therefore, genuine concern. Religion, alas, can also become narcissism, exclusively busy with itself and its own. But it is important to understand that this kind of religion, in spite of whatever Christian cloak it might be wearing, is in reality not Christianity... For the whole of Christianity consists of breaking through the terrible walls of self-centeredness, breaking through to that love which, in the words of St Paul, God has "poured into our hearts" (Rom 5:5). That is Christianity's new, eternal commandment, and the content of the entire gospel and all our faith...

20

The Samaritan Woman

Four weeks after Easter the gospel read in church is St John's account of Christ's extraordinary conversation with a Samaritan woman. According to the gospel, Christ stops at a well near the town of Sychar while his disciples go into town to buy food. A woman comes to the well to draw water, and Christ asks her to give him a drink. They strike up a conversation, and at one point the woman questions Jesus, saying, "Our fathers worshipped on this mountain, but you Jews say that Jerusalem is the place we ought to worship" (Jn 4:20). This question concerned a centuries-old argument between Jews and Samaritans, who had parted from orthodox Judaism. For the Jews, the religious center was Jerusalem; for the Samaritans it was a mountain in Samaria. Clearly, this was an argument about the external, ritual prescriptions of religion. In response, Christ tells her,

> Woman, believe me, the hour is coming when neither on this mountain nor in Jerusalem will you worship the Father...The hour is coming and now is when true worshippers will worship the Father in spirit and in truth, for such the Father seeks to worship him. God is spirit, and those who worship him must worship in spirit and in truth. (Jn 4:22-24)

There can be no doubt that these verses from John's

gospel are crucial for our understanding of Christianity. These words express and eternally proclaim a genuine religious revolution, a revolution in the very concept of religion; in these few lines, we see the birth of Christianity. In spirit and in truth! Religion, until then, and for centuries, had consisted of rules, laws, and statutes, and thus religious observance consisted entirely of blind, unquestioning submission to these rules. Not on this mountain, but in Jerusalem; not here, but there; not that way, but this way. Thus, offering to God thousands of such prescriptions, human beings protected themselves from trouble, from fear, and from painful searching. They built themselves a cage in which everything was clearly and carefully defined and there were no demands other than precise observance. And all of this is now erased and overturned in a few words: worship is not on this mountain and not in Jerusalem, but in spirit and in truth. In other terms, not in fear and blindness, not out of anxiety or distress, but in knowledge and freedom, in free choice, in love, as of a child for his father.

Now, at the center of religion, at its very heart, is not law, not submission, not prescription, but truth: "You will know the truth," Christ said, "and the truth will make you free" (Jn 8:32). At its heart now is the very process of seeking: "Seek and you will find" (Mt 7:7). Not appeasement, but thirst: "Blessed are those who hunger and thirst for righteousness" (Mt 5:6). Not slavery, but freedom: "No longer do I call you slaves, for the slave does not know what his master is doing" (Jn 15:15). Not rule-keeping, but love: "I desire mercy and not sacrifice" (Mt 9:13); "A new commandment I give to you, that you love one another; even as I have loved you, that you also love one another" (Jn 13:34).

Yes, of course, in the history of Christianity people have often forgotten Christ's words about spirit and truth and turned back to the religion of fear and ritualism, to arguments over the mountain and Jerusalem. And from outside, Christianity too often can appear to be just laws and prescriptions. But it must be judged not by externals, not by defeats and distortions, but by its inner inspiration. It must be judged on the basis of those who have accepted seriously and without any reservation these words of Christ about spirit and truth and whose whole lives have become, as it were, one continual flight of love, freedom, joy and spiritual transformation.

Despite all of its historical falls and failures, Christianity never erased these words from the gospel, and by them, therefore, it judges itself. With results much more tragic, antireligious propaganda, in its blind hatred of religion, ignores these words as if they were never said, and, to dispatch religion with greater ease, equates it with externals, superstitions and fear. Yet Christianity, first and foremost, is Christ, his teaching, the gospel. The gospel recounts how people preferred their own—their own opinions, their own ideology, their own law—to "spirit and truth," and how intolerable was this call to liberation. Here, in this story of people rejecting him who called them to live in spirit and in truth, lies the full meaning of the gospel. And thus the gospel itself gives us an explanation for that hatred of Christ which to this day forces people to lie, slander, and silently ignore.

Even now, Christianity's one threat to any ideology is this "in spirit and in truth." These words are an eternal gesture of defiance to every idol, religious or ideological; and as long as the words are not utterly uprooted from

memory, the human being will never totally accept a
teaching that enslaves him to matter and makes him nothing more than a cog in an impersonal process, a servant
to a faceless collective. And therefore, when followers of
such ideologies attack religion on grounds of stamping
out superstition, this is only for show. No, religion as
superstition, as law, as slavery, is even useful to them,
because it proves their argument. What scares them, more
than anything else in the world, is that someone will
discover the true meaning of religion, of those remarkable and liberating words of Christ: "in spirit and in
truth." Power is now on the side of militant atheism.
Religion has been gagged for almost sixty years. But this
alone proves its strength. It's voice is muzzled precisely
because within its depth it still preserves the teaching of
spirit and truth, that without spirit and truth man cannot
live, that spirit and truth are stronger than anything on
earth. The conversation that started by the well that hot
noon-day still goes on, for human beings will never stop
asking, searching, thirsting and discovering again and
again that this thirst, this seeking, this spiritual hunger
cannot be satisfied by anything but God, who is himself
Spirit and Truth, Love and Freedom, eternal Life and the
fullness of all.

21

The Lord's Ascension

There is a thrill of joy in the very word "ascension" that issues a challenge, as it were, to the so-called "laws of nature," the perpetually downward-leading, downward-pulling, and enslaving laws of gravity, weight, falling. Here, in contrast, all is lightness, flight, an endless soaring upward. The Lord's Ascension is celebrated forty days after Easter, on Thursday of the sixth week after the feast of Christ's Resurrection.

On Wednesday, the day before, what in church practice is known as the "leave-taking of Pascha" takes place, as if to say farewell to Easter. From beginning to end the service is celebrated exactly as it was on the night of Easter itself, with the singing of the same joyful verses: "Let God arise, let His enemies be scattered...," "This is the day which the Lord has made, let us rejoice and be glad in it..." Chanting these verses, the priest holds the paschal candle and censes the whole church, while "Christ is Risen" rings out in response. We part with Easter, we "take leave" for another year.

It seems that we should feel sad. But instead of sadness, we are sent new joy: the joy of contemplating and celebrating the Ascension. In the gospel account of this event, after the Lord had given his final instructions to the

disciples, He "led them out as far as Bethany, and lifting up
his hands He blessed them. While he blessed them he parted
from them, and was carried into heaven. And they worshipped him, and returned to Jerusalem with great joy..."
(Lk 24:50-52). "With great joy..." What is the source of this
great joy that endures to this day and explodes with such
remarkable brightness on the feast of Ascension? For it
seems that Christ went away and left his disciples alone; it
was a day of separation. Ahead of them lies the long, long
road of preaching, persecution, suffering, and temptation
that fills to overflowing the history of Christianity and the
Church. The joy had apparently come to an end, the joy of
earthly and daily fellowship with Christ, the protection of
his power and divinity. But how rightly one pastor entitled
his sermon on Ascension as "the joy of separation"! For, of
course, the church is not celebrating Christ's departure.
Christ said: "I am with you always until the close of the age"
(Mt 28:20), and the entire joy of Christian faith is in the
awareness of his presence, just as he promised: "Where two
or three are gathered in my name, there am I in the midst of
them" (Mt 18:20). We celebrate not Christ's departure, but
his ascension into heaven.

The feast of the Ascension is the celebration of
heaven now opened to human beings, heaven as the new
and eternal home, heaven as our true homeland. Sin sev-
ered earth from heaven and made us earthly and coarse, it
fixed our gaze solidly on the ground and made our life
exclusively earthbound. Sin is the betrayal of heaven in
the soul. It is precisely on this day, on the feast of the
Ascension, that we cannot fail to be horrified by this
renunciation that fills the whole world. With self-impor-
tance and pride, man announces that he is strictly mate-

rial, that the whole world is material, and that there is nothing beyond the material. And for some reason he is even glad about this, and speaks with pity and condescension, as he would of buffoons and boors, of those who still believe in some sort of "heaven." Come on brothers, heaven is the sky, it's just as material as everything else; there is nothing else, there never was and never will be. We die, we disappear; so in the meantime, let's build an earthly paradise and forget about the fantasies of priests. This in brief, but absolutely accurately, is the end result and high-point of our culture, our science, our ideology. Progress ends in the cemetery, with the progress of worms feeding on corpses. But what do you propose, they ask us, what is this heaven you talk about, into which Christ ascended? After all, up in the sky nothing of what you are speaking exists.

Let the answer to this question come from John Chrysostom, a Christian preacher who lived sixteen centuries ago. Speaking about heaven, he exclaims: "What need do I have for heaven, when I myself will become heaven..." Let the answer come from our ancestors, who called the church "heaven on earth." The essential point of both these answers is this: heaven is the name of our authentic vocation as human beings, heaven is the final truth about the earth. No, heaven is not somewhere in outer space beyond the planets, or in some unknown galaxy. Heaven is what Christ gives back to us, what we lost through our sin and pride, through our earthly, exclusively earthly, sciences and ideologies, and now it is opened, offered, and returned to us by Christ. Heaven is the kingdom of eternal life, the kingdom of truth, goodness and beauty. Heaven is the total spiritual transformation of human life; heaven is the kingdom of God, victory over death, the triumph of love and care; heaven is the fulfillment of that ultimate desire, about which it was said: "Eye has not seen, nor ear heard, nor has it entered into the heart of man, what God has prepared for those who love him" (1 Cor 2:9). All of this is revealed to us, all of this is given to us by Christ. And therefore, heaven permeates our life here and now, the earth itself becomes a reflection, a mirror image of heavenly beauty. Who descended from heaven to earth to return heaven to us? God. Who ascended from earth to heaven? The man Jesus.

St Athanasius the Great says that "God became man so that man could become God." God came down to earth so that we might ascend to heaven! This is what the Ascension celebrates! This is the source of its brightness and unspeakable joy. If Christ is in heaven, and if we believe in him and love him, then we also are there with him, at his banquet, in his Kingdom. If humanity ascends through him, and does not fall, then through him, I also have access to ascension and am called to him. And in him, the goal, meaning and ultimate joy of my life is revealed to me. Everything, everything around us pulls us down. But I look at the divine flesh ascending to heaven, at Christ going up "with the sound of a trumpet," and I say to myself and to the world: here is the truth about the world and humanity, here is the life to which God calls us from all eternity.

> Completing Your whole plan for us,
> Uniting earth to heaven,
> You ascended in glory, O Christ God,
> Not parting at all,
> But ever remaining,
> And saying to those who love You:
> I am with you and no one will be against you...

22

Pentecost

"The feast of the descent of the Holy Spirit." I say these words I've known since childhood, and all at once they strike me as if I'm hearing them for the first time. Yes, from the time I was a child I knew that ten days following the Ascension, meaning fifty days after Pascha, Christians from time immemorial celebrated and continue to celebrate the descent of the Holy Spirit in a feast known by its church name as Pentecost, or more popularly as "Trinity," the day of the Trinity.

For centuries, to prepare for this feast the churches were cleaned and adorned with greenery and branches, and grass was strewn about the floor... On the day of the feast, at the solemn vespers, the faithful stood in church holding flowers in their hands. These customs explain how the feast of Pentecost entered Russian popular consciousness and literature as a kind of sun-filled, bright celebration, the feast of flowering, a kind of joyful encounter between human beings and God's world in all its beauty and grace.

All religions, including the most ancient and primitive, had a feast of summer flowering, a feast to celebrate the first appearance of shoots, plants, fruit. In ancient Judaism, this was the feast of Pentecost. If in Old Testament religion Passover celebrated spring's resurrection of the world and nature, then the Jewish Pentecost was the feast of movement from spring to summer, celebrating the victory of sun and light, the feast of cosmic fulness. But in the Old Testament a feast common to all human societies acquires a new meaning: it becomes the annual commemoration of the ascent of Moses up Mount Sinai, where in an inexpressible mystical encounter God revealed himself, entered into a Covenant, gave commandments, and promised salvation. In other terms, religion ceased being simply nature, and now became the beginning of history: God had revealed his law, his commandments, his plan for humanity, and had shown the way. Spring, summer, the eternal natural cycle, became a sign and symbol not only of nature, but of man's spiritual destiny and the commandment to grow into fullness of knowledge, life and perfect wholeness... Finally, in the very last phase of the Old Testament, through the teaching and insight of the prophets, this feast became a celebration directed toward the future, to God's final victory in his creation. Here is how the prophet Joel speaks of this:

> And it shall come to pass afterward that I will pour out my spirit on all flesh; your sons and your daughters shall prophesy, your old men shall dream dreams, and your young men shall see visions. Even upon the menservants and maidservants in those days, I will pour out my spirit. And I will give signs in the heavens and on the earth...before the great and terrible day of the Lord comes. And it shall come to pass that all who call upon the name of the Lord shall be delivered... (Joel 2:28-32)

Thus, the Jewish feast of Pentecost is a feast of nature and the cosmos, a feast of history as the revelation of

God's will for the world and human beings, a feast of future triumph, of God's victory over evil and the coming of the great and last "day of the Lord." All this must be kept in mind in order to grasp how the first Christians experienced, understood, and celebrated their feast of Pentecost, and why it became one of the most important Christian celebrations.

The Book of Acts, devoted to recounting the history of the first Christians and the initial spread of Christianity, starts precisely with the day of Pentecost, describing what took place fifty days after Christ's resurrection and ten days after his ascension into heaven. Just before his ascension Christ had told the disciples "not to depart from Jerusalem, but to wait for the promise of the Father, which he said, 'you heard from me...'" (Acts 1:4). So in ten days, according to St Luke's account,

> When the day of Pentecost had come, they were all together in one place. And suddenly a sound came from heaven like the rush of a mighty wind, and it filled all the house where they were sitting. And there appeared to them tongues as of fire, distributed and resting on each one of them. And they were all filled with the Holy Spirit and began to speak in other tongues, as the Spirit gave them utterance... And all who heard were amazed and perplexed, saying to one another, "What does this mean?" But others mocking said, "They are filled with new wine." (Acts 2:1-4, 12-13)

To those witnesses who remained skeptical, the apostle Peter explained the meaning of the event using the words of the prophet Joel quoted above. "This is what was spoken by the prophet Joel," he said, "'And in the last days it shall be, God declares, that I will pour out my Spirit on all flesh...'" (Acts 2:16,17).

For the Christian, therefore, the feast of Pentecost is the completion of all that Christ accomplished. Christ taught about the Kingdom of God, and here it is, now opened! Christ promised that the Spirit of God would reveal the truth, and now this is fulfilled. The world, history, life, time, are all illumined with the final, transcendent light—all are filled with ultimate meaning. The last and great day of the Lord has begun!

23

The Transfiguration

Everlasting Light

Transfiguration! What a wonderful, beautiful and joyous word this is! It reverberates in soul and mind with such brightness and celebration! For centuries the Russian people loved this summer, August feast of the Lord's Transfiguration, when, in the words of Fedor Tiutchev, "it is as if the whole day becomes crystal-clear and radiant."

What is this feast about, what is its essence and the source of its joy and light? First, let's hear the gospel narrative of the event. Jesus, according to the account in St Matthew's gospel,

took with him Peter and James and John his brother, and led them up a high mountain apart. And He was transfigured before them, and his face shone like the sun, and his garments became white as light. And behold, there appeared to them Moses and Elijah, talking with him. And Peter said to Jesus, "Lord, it is good for us to be here; if you wish, I will make three booths here"... He was still speaking, when lo, a bright cloud overshadowed them, and a voice from the cloud said, "This is my beloved Son, with whom I am well pleased; listen to him." When the disciples heard this, they fell on their faces, and were filled with awe. But Jesus came

and touched them, saying, "Rise, and have no fear." And
when they lifted up their eyes, they saw no one but Jesus
only. And as they were coming down the mountain,
Jesus commanded them, "Tell no one the vision, until
the Son of man is raised from the dead." (Mt 17:1-9)

What does this gospel story mean? What place does this
enigmatic revelation of glory have in the earthly life and work
of Christ?

Few would disagree Christ's image in the gospels is
first and foremost an image of humility. Beginning with
his birth, there was no room to be found in any of the
homes in the town, and so He was born outside, in a cave.
And to the very end He was without a home, "having no
place"—as He himself said—"to lay his head" (Mt 8:20).
Those whom He healed and helped He commanded to tell
no one. He shunned all honors and every opportunity for
fame. And He voluntarily left the safety of Galilee, where
there was no threat, and chose to return to Jerusalem,
where what awaited him was suffering, the humiliation of
a trial and judgment, and a painful, shameful execution.
"Learn from me," He said, "for I am meek and lowly of
heart..." (Mt 11:29).

In this life of humility and self-renunciation, there
were only a few occasions when the hidden rays of divine
power and glory broke through. But, without exception,
only a very few people witnessed these "glorifications,"
and even they usually did not comprehend the significance of what they saw. This is how it was on the night of
his birth, when simple shepherds heard the angels' hymn
of glory, the "tidings," as the gospel says, "of great joy"
(Lk 2:10). This is how it was, already many years later,
on the day Jesus came to accept baptism in the Jordan,

when we hear that same voice from heaven and the same words heard at the Transfiguration: "This is my beloved Son..." (Mt 3:17). Finally, He is glorified here on the mountain, in the presence of the three disciples. And every time this mysterious heavenly glory is revealed, the glorification comes not from human beings, but from above, from heaven. The Church answers, and has always answered, the question about the meaning of Christ's earthly glorification not with explanations but by celebrations—by celebration of that unique joy that marks the annual commemoration of the Transfiguration.

One word dominates this feast in all its prayers, hymns and readings. This word is light. "Let your everlasting light shine also upon us sinners." The world is a dark, cold and terrifying place. And this darkness is not dispelled by the physical light of the sun. On the contrary, perhaps, the sun's light makes human life seem even more terrible and hopeless as life surges relentlessly and inexorably, bound by sufferings and loneliness, toward death and annihilation. All is condemned, all suffers, all is subject to the incomprehensible and merciless law of sin and death. But then comes the appearance on earth, the entrance into the world, of a man, humble and homeless, who has no authority at all over anyone, who has no earthly power whatsoever. And He tells people that this kingdom of darkness, evil and death is not our true life; that this is not the world God created; that evil and suffering and finally death itself can and must be conquered; and that He is sent by God, his own Father, to save people from this terrible bondage to sin and death.

Human beings have forgotten their true nature and calling, renounced them. They must turn to see that they have lost the ability to see, to hear what they are already incapable of hearing. They must come to believe all over again that good is stronger than evil, love stronger than hate, life stronger than death. Christ heals, helps and gives himself to everyone. And nevertheless the people do not understand, do not hear, do not believe. He could have revealed his divine glory and power and forced them to believe in him. But He wants from them only freely-given faith, freely-given love, freely-given acceptance. He knows that in the hour of his ultimate sacrifice, ultimate self-giving, everyone will flee in fear and forsake him. But right now, so that afterwards, when everything is finished, the world would still have some evidence of where He is inviting people to come, what He is offering us as a gift, as life, as the fullness of meaning and joy; now, therefore, hidden from the world and from the people, He reveals to three of his own disciples that glory, that light, that victorious celebration to which man is called from eternity.

The divine light, permeating the entire world. The divine light, transfiguring man. The divine light in which everything acquires its ultimate and eternal meaning. "It is good for us to be here," cried the apostle Peter seeing this light and this glory. And from that time, Christianity, the Church, faith is one continuous, joyful repetition of this "it is good for us to be here." But faith is also a plea for the everlasting light, a thirst for this illumination and transfiguration. This light continues to shine, through the darkness and evil, through the drab grayness and dull routine of this world, like a ray of sun piercing through the clouds. It is recognized by the soul, it comforts the heart, it makes us feel alive, and it transfigures us from within.

"Lord! It is good for us to be here!" If only these words might become ours, if only they might become our soul's answer to the gift of divine light, if only our prayer might become the prayer for transfiguration, for the victory of light! "Let your everlasting light shine also upon us sinners!"

The Blessing of Fruit

It is an ancient custom in Orthodox churches to bless fruits and vegetables on the feast of Transfiguration. This prompts us to ask ourselves: what is the meaning of this ancient rite, and of blessing, sanctification in general, since the blessing of fruit on Transfiguration is only one of many such rites? If we open the liturgical service book where all these rites are collected, the so-called "Book of Needs," we find special services such as blessings for a new home, a field, a garden, a well. It is as if the Church addresses itself to the entire world, as if God's right hand of blessing were being extended over all through these rites of blessing and sanctification. Why have people from time immemorial felt the need for blessings?

We must say immediately that proponents of anti-religious propaganda unquestioningly regard all these rites as superstition which, in their view, is the whole content of religion. They argue that superstition is a product of fear: a person is afraid of being poisoned, afraid of a bad harvest, afraid that his house will burn down, afraid of other people. Religion purveys deliverance from fear: sprinkle the fruit or the garden or the home with holy water and God will protect both them and you. "So you see, it's all crude ignorance, superstition and...deception." However, in presenting the issue this way, atheist propaganda does not mention any of the prayers or rites involved with these supposed superstitions. They make it sound as if priests, the clergy, are a cadre of swindlers who exploit fear and ignorance by using incomprehensible magical incantations. But if one actually listens to these prayers and looks closely at these rites, if only once in a lifetime one experiences the joy of that radiant and sunlit Transfiguration noonday blessing, then it becomes clear that the deception is not coming from the Church, but from ill-willed atheist propaganda. It is precisely this propaganda, and not the Church's prayer, which is permeated with fear, mistrust, and a need to denounce anything more elevated, more pure, more profound than its own simplistic, mundane, and materialistic approach to the world and to life. For what we see and hear and experience above all in these rites and prayers is joy and thanksgiving. But if fear were present, there could be no joy and no thanksgiving; and conversely, if joy is present, there can be no fear. Fear produces misery and mistrust, but there is none of this in transfiguration's light. But what is the source of this joy and thanksgiving?

One of Osip Mandelshtam's poems, devoted to the eucharistic liturgy, the main service of Christian worship, includes this wonderful verse: "Take into your hands the whole world, as if it were a simple apple..." Perhaps here, because it is so simple and childlike, we see better than anywhere else the source of joy and thanksgiving that permeate Christian faith. In an apple, and in everything within the world, faith sees, recognizes, and accepts God's gift, filled with love, beauty and wisdom. Faith hears the apple and the world speaking of that boundless love that created the world and life and gave them to us as our life. The world itself is the fruit of God's love for humanity, and only through the world can human beings recognize God and love him in return... And only in truly loving his own life, can a person thereby accept the life of the world as God's gift. Our fall, our sin, is that we take everything for granted—and therefore everything, including ourselves, becomes routine, depressing, empty. The apple becomes just an apple. Bread is just bread. A human being is just a human being. We know their weight, their appearance, their activities, we know everything about them, but we no longer know them, because we do not see the light that shines through them. The eternal task of faith and of the Church is to overcome this sinful, monotonous habituation; to enable us to see once again what we have forgotten how to see; to feel what we no longer feel; to experience what we are no longer capable of experiencing. Thus, the priest blesses bread and wine, lifting them up to heaven, but faith sees the bread of life, it sees sacrifice and gift, it sees communion with life eternal.

So, on Transfiguration we bring to church apples, pears, grapes, vegetables, and suddenly the church itself is transformed anew into that mystical garden, into that blessed paradise where man's life and his encounter with God began. And just as that first man rejoiced and gave thanks to God as he opened his eyes for the first time and saw this world where everything, by God's own word, was "very good," so in this rite of blessing we see the world as if for the first time, as the reflection of God's wisdom and love, and we rejoice and give thanks. And through this joy and thanksgiving our life is purified, renewed and reborn. No, we do not negate the material world, as atheist propaganda falsely claims, nor do we repudiate it; on the contrary, we sanctify and bless it, for in it we joyfully and with thanksgiving see and feel the gift of God. "Heaven and earth are full of your glory," we sing in church. The significance of blessing is that through it, this glory breaks into our drowsy consciousness, opens our ears, opens our eyes, and life itself becomes praise, joy and thanksgiving.

But what about evil, people ask me. What about suffering, what about death? To this we answer: if we are filled to the brim with this light, if we genuinely accept this blessing and sanctification and bring them within, then we ourselves become the place where the victory over evil begins. And death will be swallowed up in victory, for we live in a world where Christ lived and continues forever to be present. And if in everything and everyone in the world we see him, love him, give ourselves to him; if in all, we see the light of his presence, his love, and his victory—then nothing can separate us from him.